CULTURES OF THE WORLD

PAKISTAN

Sean Sheehan

MARSHALL CAVENDISH
New York • London • Sydney

Reference edition published 1994 by
Marshall Cavendish Corporation
2415 Jerusalem Avenue
P.O. Box 587
North Bellmore
New York 11710

© Times Editions Pte Ltd 1994

Originated and designed by
Times Books International, an imprint of
Times Editions Pte Ltd

Printed in Singapore

Library of Congress Cataloging-in-Publication Data:
Sheehan, Sean.
    Pakistan / Sean Sheehan.
        p. cm.—(Cultures Of The World)
    Includes bibliographical references and index.
    Summary: Explores in text and photographs the
    geography, history, government, economy, and
    culture of this nation in South Asia.
    ISBN 1-85435-583-X
    1. Pakistan—Juvenile literature [1. Pakistan.]
I. Title. II. Series.
DS376.9.S49 1993
954.91—dc20   93–4379
                    CIP
                    AC

Cultures of the World

Editorial Director	Shirley Hew
Managing Editor	Shova Loh
Editors	Michael Spilling
	Winnifred Wong
	Falak Kagda
	Roslind Varghese
	Jenny Goh
	Sue Sismondo
Picture Editor	Yee May Kaung
Production	Edmund Lam
Design	Tuck Loong
	Ronn Yeo
	Felicia Wong
	Loo Chuan Ming
Illustrators	Jimmy Kang
	Andrew Leong
	Anuar bin Abdul Rahim
MCC Editorial Director	Evelyn M. Fazio

INTRODUCTION

 MANY OF THE CATCH PHRASES that have become misleading clichés in travel brochures are lived out in Pakistan. The country and its peoples are truly diverse and fascinating. There is a potpourri of cultures that have little in common. Nomadic tribes in Sindh still collect roots and berries, while the hill Pathans carry and use their guns and knives with a code of honor that would have impressed medieval knights and heroes of the American Wild West. On the other hand, Lahore churns out movies regularly.

Despite the exotic diversity, Pakistan is a country unified by religion. It was born of a need for Moslems in India to have a country of their own. Pakistan came into existence in 1947 amid one of the bloodiest conflicts of the 20th century. Its political situation since then has continued to be full of conflicts, with elected leaders being deposed every few years.

Pakistan has been called "a castle with a thousand doors," and this book sets out to open some of these doors. Its history and geography, languages and lifestyles, habits of dress and thought, and much else, are dealt with in words and pictures that bring to life a most fascinating country.

CONTENTS

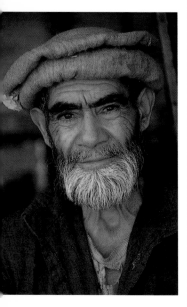

A rural Hunza man.

CONTENTS

Two Kalash girls.

5

GEOGRAPHY

PAKISTAN is a country in the northwest of the Indian subcontinent. To the east and southeast is India, to the west is Iran, and to the north are Afghanistan, the former Soviet Union, and China. Mountains stretch down to the Arabian Sea and below them is the broad valley of the Indus River. There are four distinct areas: Punjab, Sindh, Balochistan, and the North West Frontier Province. Four tributaries of the mighty Indus water the plateau of the Punjab, the area of Pakistan most blessed by nature. Other regions of the country, Balochistan for example, are different in character and impose harsher conditions on the people who live there. The regional differences in landscape and fertility of the soil mirror the differences of the peoples who live off the land.

Opposite: **Spectacular scenery like this view of the Shegar Valley are plentiful in Pakistan.**

Below: **Terraced hills, to maximize agricultural use of the land, are a common sight.**

7

MOUNTAINS

The Karakoram range boasts K2 and Nanga Parbat, the second and third highest mountain peaks in the world.

Three great mountain ranges make their presence felt in Pakistan: the Himalayas, the Karakorams, and the Hindu Kush. The Himalayas form the highest mountain system in the world. Two hundred and fifty of the world's highest peaks are found in Pakistan.

The Karakoram chain of mountains stretches for about 300 miles and contains 60 peaks that rise over 22,000 feet. Most of Pakistan's highest mountains are part of the Karakorams and are to be found near the disputed Kashmir border with India. All the mountain passes are perpetually snow-covered, but this has not prevented them from providing a passageway between Pakistan and Kashmir or China.

The Hindu Kush range of mountains stretches for about 500 miles along Pakistan's border with Afghanistan. These mountains are permanently covered with snow. This is where the famous Khyber Pass, linking Pakistan and Afghanistan, can be found.

Mountaineers are fascinated by the challenge of scaling the high peaks of all three ranges, and Pakistan provides many of the people who form part of any climbing expedition. Some are just porters, carrying supplies to base camps from which the real climbing begins, but others are professionals in their own right. They accompany the climbers and provide invaluable information and assistance in coping with the rigors of the high-altitude environment. During the winter months, the snow freezes into a slippery, icy mass, making climbing impossible, and it is usually in mid-April that the mountaineering season gets under way. Even then the temperature drops to below freezing above 2,000 feet, and there is a danger of frostbite although the sun may be shining brightly overhead.

THE CHALLENGE OF K2

Rising in splendid isolation at the head of the 55-mile-long Baltoro Glacier, K2 is the second-highest mountain peak in the world. At 28,250 feet, it is only 778 feet lower than Mt. Everest. Recent satellite evidence suggests it might be higher than previously thought, and there has been speculation that K2 might even be higher than Everest.

K2 was previously called Godwin-Austen, after the eldest son of an English geologist, but this name was never officially recognized. The mountain was named K2 because it was the second to be measured in the Karakorams.

K2 is considered by most professional mountaineers to be far more difficult to climb than Everest, and many consider it virtually unscalable. Before 1954 there had been five expeditions on K2, all failing to reach the summit. Two of the five expeditions resulted in several deaths.

Despite such dangers, an Italian team conquered K2 on August 31, 1954. Then, in 1986, nine expeditions converged on the mountain and seven climbers, including the first woman, reached the summit. Tragedy, however, took its toll and 13 people died that year on K2, including the seven who had reached the summit.

The fertile Indus Plain has made Punjab and Sindh the breadbowl of the country.

THE INDUS PLAIN

The Indus Plain is a vast region of some 200,000 square miles and constitutes the most prosperous agricultural region of Pakistan. The province of Punjab is in the northern part of this area. The literal meaning of "Punjab" is "the five waters," referring to the fact that five important tributaries of the Indus flow through Punjab (now divided between India and Pakistan so that one tributary is in India) and provide an invaluable supply of water. The greatest concentration of the country's population lives in Punjab, and Islamabad, the nation's capital, lies in this region.

The areas between the streams of water are known as *doabs* ("DOH-hb") and improved irrigation techniques have made most of them very rich agriculturally. Pakistan has the largest artificial irrigation system in the world. The irrigation, however, is causing problems in the form of waterlogged soil and excessive salinity. The rate of evaporation is greater than the rate of rainfall, and therefore mineral salts accumulate in the

THE RIVER INDUS

Ancient works of Indian literature, written when Pakistan did not yet exist as a separate state, refer to the Indus as "King River," and today it is indisputably the great waterway of Pakistan. Its journey of 1,700 miles begins in Tibet, where it starts as little more than melting ice from the glaciers of the Himalayas. Each summer, the heat from the sun melts so much ice that the river swells and overflows as it winds its way south. The rich alluvial plains of Punjab and Sindh are largely formed by the fertile silt deposited by the Indus and its tributaries.

Farther south, the river enters a narrow gorge. It is here that it can most easily be harnessed for irrigation. Indeed, so much water is removed from the Indus for irrigation that big boats can no longer use the river, although small boats can navigate the final stage of the river's journey to the Arabian Sea.

With the help of modern technology, Pakistan is exploiting the river's value as a source of power and irrigation. Large dams have been constructed to hold back the summer floods and release the waters later into the numerous irrigation canals that now dot the landscape of Punjab and Sindh. Hydroelectric plants are also being constructed along the river in order to provide electricity for the industrial centers and towns of the Indus Plain.

water. As the salts find their way into the land, they slow down plant growth and increase the likelihood of the soil becoming infertile. Pakistan's scientists are working on ways to neutralize the salinity; they are also working on developing a hardy wheat hybrid that will thrive in saline soil.

The four tributaries join the Indus in east-central Pakistan, and the southern part of the Indus Plain is known as the province of Sindh. The problem of salinity is more severe in Sindh than in any other region of the country.

BALOCHISTAN

This large province in west and southwest Pakistan occupies an area of over 134,000 square miles. It is separated from the Indus Plain by mountains and is generally a high and rocky area averaging over 1,000 feet in elevation. Despite this inhospitable geography, the Balochis manage to survive due to a unique system of irrigation known as the *karez* ("kah-REZ"). At the foot of the rocky hills, water is collected in underground canals and carried to neighboring fields, where it is drawn off by strategically located well shafts. The underground canals minimize water loss through evaporation due to the dry climate. Farmers manage to grow some crops and supplement this by rearing sheep and goats.

The hardy Balochis valiantly eke out a living from their inhospitable land.

CLIMATE

The amount of rainfall in Pakistan varies not only from region to region, but also—because of the unpredictability of droughts and monsoons—from year to year. "Monsoon" originally described a wind over the Arabian Sea but is now used to describe the rainy seasons of east Asia and Africa. The vast land mass warms up during the summer, and as the warm air rises, the air pressure is reduced. Warm, moist air from the oceans is then drawn in by the seasonal wind. It rains mostly from May to September. Eastern Punjab receives 20 inches of rain a year, while most of Balochistan receives less than five inches a year. The heaviest rains fall near the high mountains in the north. Annual rainfall here can be as much as 35 inches a year.

Hot, rainy summers and long, cold winters are the norm. In the north, summer temperatures average 75°F, and in the winter freezing temperatures are common. In Punjab and Sindh, summer temperatures average 90°F, falling to 55°F in winter. Balochistan experiences similar temperatures, generally about 10°F less than Punjab.

The faster the warm, moist air is forced to rise, the shorter and heavier the rain showers become. Not surprisingly, then, the mountainous region in the north of the country experiences the highest rainfall.

The jasmine is Pakistan's national flower. It is common to most parts of the country and can be found in elegant gardens as well as villages. The jasmine, a simple white flower, is admired for its beauty and especially for its fragrance, which is thought to soothe the mind. The Moghul emperors were very fond of jasmine and planted huge groves of it in their gardens.

FLORA AND FAUNA

The most exciting wildlife is found in the North West Frontier Province, where bears and leopards still roam. This is where the increasingly rare snow leopard—also known as the clouded leopard because its thick, pale grey, dark-ringed coat looks like clouds—can still be found living in the forests near the snow line. The clouded leopard is a protected species as only about 250 remain.

Another protected species is the bustard. The bustard, a fowl, was a popular food source and was excessively hunted until it was in danger of extinction. With the help of the World Wildlife Fund, the government is preserving the species.

Around the southern delta area crocodiles and pythons are common. Also found here is the Indus River dolphin, which is blind and navigates by sonar. It is also a protected species.

The dry climate and the hot summers determine the plant life to a large extent. Apart from plantations and orchards, trees are not very common; low-lying bushes are more likely to be seen in the landscape. Typical vegetation consists of short grass, and in Balochistan only xerophytic plants—plants adapted to hot, dry climates—are likely to survive. The Thar Desert (also known as the Great Indian Desert) covers part of east Pakistan and, although it contains patches of clay, across the tracts of pure sand there is virtually no vegetation.

CITIES

The majority of Pakistanis live in the countryside, but there are a dozen cities with populations exceeding 200,000. Islamabad is the capital, but the largest center of population is concentrated in Karachi, where over five million people live. Situated on the Arabian Sea, Karachi was regarded as an inconvenient center for the federal government, so a commission was set up in 1959 to choose a site for a new city. Construction began two years later, and in 1964 the first inhabitants, mostly civil servants, moved into their new homes in Islamabad.

Islamabad is not like any other city in Pakistan, or even in Asia. Having been planned from scratch, it exhibits little of the haphazard development that characterizes many Asian cities. More than six million trees have been planted and most buildings are low-level, two-story constructions. Islamabad offers a complete contrast to Rawalpindi, a neighboring city about eight miles to the south, which was founded in the 14th century by the Moghuls and developed by the British in the 19th century. Rawalpindi is a noisy, bustling place, typical of Pakistan's urban centers, and the city's bazaars attract traders from neighboring Kashmir and beyond.

A busy highway connects Islamabad and Rawalpindi, also known as just 'Pindi, and the long-term plan is for both cities to develop into a massive twin-city metropolis sharing urban services and amenities.

Unlike most cities in Asia, which mushroomed haphazardly around rivers or deltas, the site for Islamabad was selected by a committee and planned in an orderly fashion.

HISTORY

THE HISTORY OF PAKISTAN unfolds into a dramatic canvas of events that features some of the world's greatest empires. Iranian, Greek, Turkish, Moghul, and British imperialists have fought over the land, established their cultures, and then faded away as new forces made their presence felt. Yet the country where these civilizations flourished and then floundered did not come into existence as a separate nation until 1947. Until then, the country known today as Pakistan was part of India. The years since 1947 have been equally eventful and turbulent, and, if anything, even more dramatic.

Opposite: **The mausoleum of Muhammad Ali Jinnah, the founder of modern Pakistan.**

Below: **A view of the main bath at Mohenjo-Daro, a civilization that flourished along the Indus River 5,000 years ago.**

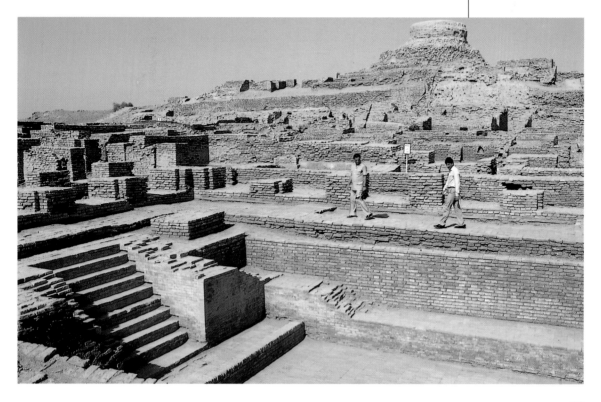

THE INDUS VALLEY CIVILIZATION

Recently, evidence of an 8,000-year-old civilization was unearthed in Balochistan. If confirmed by experts, this would be the oldest civilization yet unearthed.

Archeologists began to unearth evidence of this great civilization during the 1920s. Digging began around two town sites—Mohenjo-Daro on the Indus River and Harappa on a tributary of the same river—and what came to light revealed a culture that extended for some 1,000 miles, making it by far the largest of the world's first civilizations. It is sometimes referred to as the Harappan civilization.

The Indus Valley civilization flourished about 4,500 years ago, although its origins remain unclear. Historians speculate that nomadic tribes settled along the river plain, perhaps imitating the successful agriculture begun by earlier, more dispersed farming communities. Undoubtedly, the cycle of the Indus was crucial, for as the water receded each summer, the alluvial soil left behind provided a rich earth for agriculture without the need for plowing or manuring. How this farming lifestyle evolved into a mature and sophisticated culture remains a mystery. While there is some evidence suggesting force was employed, it is also likely that the period of development was a slow and mainly peaceful process.

Tangible evidence provides proof of an impressive society. Animals were domesticated, crops harvested and stored, copper mined, and streets laid out on a grid pattern resembling that of a modern city in the United States. Houses were constructed of red bricks, and unlike other early civilizations—such as the Nile Valley civilization in Egypt—the extent of urban planning suggests that houses were not just for the privileged few but were inhabited by the bulk of the population. An extensive drainage system and the use of a uniform

system of weights and measures support the idea that a central authority planned and coordinated matters of public interest.

The communities of the Indus Valley did not live in splendid isolation. Trade was conducted with south India, Afghanistan, Arabia, and Central Asia, and there is evidence to suggest that sea trade facilitated the exchange of goods and raw materials with Mesopotamia, another great civilization then developing between the Euphrates and Tigris rivers in the Middle East.

This highly developed urban civilization came to an abrupt end around 1500 B.C., and scholars have speculated about the causes of its decline. Invasion, catastrophe, and overpopulation have all been advanced as possible factors, but conclusive proof continues to elude researchers. What is certain is that the end came suddenly. Towns were abandoned and the people probably returned to a nomadic form of life. An inspiring experiment in urban planning, a settled agriculture, and a peaceful existence came to an inexplicable end.

While excavations are continuing to reveal the immense complexity and sophistication of the Indus Valley civilization, there are still many unanswered questions, and their script remains undeciphered.

Opposite: **Many steatite seals, like this one found at Harappa, depict bulls and have formal pictorial symbols written from right to left.**

This bridge of boats spanning the mighty Indus River is the only mark Alexander the Great left on Pakistan.

THE ARYANS AND AFTER

From Persia, the Aryans arrived in what is now Pakistan around 1400 B.C., although scholars tend not to associate them with the decline of the Indus Valley civilization. Little archeological evidence of their presence remains, although their written scripts are important sources for the origin of the Indian caste system and Hindu religious beliefs.

Alexander the Great crossed the Hindu Kush in 327 B.C., but his battle-weary troops were not inclined to travel further east, so he sailed down to the Indus delta and from there returned to Babylon, where he died in 323 B.C.

In the centuries that followed, many peoples from different parts of Asia occupied what is now Pakistan: the Indians from the Mauryan empire, the Greeks of Bactria, the Huns, the Arab Moslems in A.D. 711, and then the Turks, followed much later by the mighty Moghuls.

THE MOGHUL EMPIRE

By the early 16th century, the Moghuls, with an army of elephants and matchlocks, had established control over northern India and what is now Pakistan. The first Moghul emperor was Babur (1483–1530), whose military genius initiated some 200 years of Moghul rule. He possessed a love of learning and was an enlightened ruler. His son Humayun (1508–1556) lacked the energy and vision of his father but was responsible for introducing aspects of Persian art and the Persian language into the Moghul domain. The culture of Pakistan was significantly affected by the Moghuls.

Shah Jehan built the Taj Mahal in memory of his beloved wife Mumtaz Mahal, and is buried there beside her.

The next Moghul emperor was Akbar (1542–1605). Generally considered the greatest of the Moghuls, Akbar ruled for nearly 50 years. The Moghul empire was firmly established during this time, and after 1585 Akbar moved his capital from near Agra in India to Lahore, now in Pakistan, where he built the magnificent Lahore Fort.

Akbar was succeeded by Jahangir (1605–1627), famous for his encouragement of the arts and equally infamous for his cruelty and addiction to drugs and alcohol. After his death, his son Shah Jehan (1592–1666) became emperor and has been immortalized as the spirit behind the building of the Taj Mahal in India. Shah Jehan actually died in prison, put there by his son Aurangzeb (1618–1707), who was the last Moghul emperor.

PAKISTAN AND THE BRITISH

The British badges carved into the rocks near the Khyber Pass are a reminder that the British Empire once extended to this part of the world.

Soon after Vasco da Gama discovered a sea route to India in 1498, European traders began to make their presence felt in Asia. The East India Company was founded by British merchants in 1600, and over the next two and a half centuries the company gradually extended its control through military and political means. By the time the company was disbanded in 1858, Punjab and Sindh had become part of British India, the jewel in the crown of the British empire.

The North West Frontier Province and Balochistan were highly valued as buffer states against Russia, and by the beginning of the 20th century the whole of what is now Pakistan was part of British India.

Many historians attribute the creation of Pakistan to the policies of the British in India. The spread of Western education, in particular, had the effect of alienating Moslems, who were more inclined to insist on their own religious schools than Hindus. At the same time, the British were willing to exploit the religious differences in order to weaken the threat posed by the Indians' demand for self-government.

By the end of World War II, independence for India was inevitable, but the British had come to think that an independent Moslem state was also inevitable. In 1946, 5,000 people died during religious conflicts in the city of Calcutta. The pressure for a new Moslem state was spearheaded by Muhammad Ali Jinnah, a man whose name is inseparable from the birth of Pakistan.

MUHAMMAD ALI JINNAH (1875–1948)

When Muhammad Ali Jinnah joined the Indian National Congress as a young man, the congress represented both Hindu and Moslem aspirations for self-determination. At first Jinnah was an ardent supporter of Hindu-Moslem unity, but he became disillusioned with Mohandas Gandhi's leadership of the Congress, and in 1930 he left for England. By the time he returned in 1934, he had abandoned the idea of Hindu-Moslem unity and was stridently advocating a separate home for India's Moslems.

Jinnah campaigned for an independent Pakistan, which means "the land of the pure" in Urdu. The big problem was how to determine which parts of India would become Pakistan. "I don't care how little you give me," Jinnah said to the British, "as long as you give it to me completely."

When Jinnah's Pakistan emerged into history in 1947, it was unique, consisting of two parts separated by 1,000 miles of Indian territory. In the northwest, Sindh, Punjab, the North West Frontier Province, and Balochistan became West Pakistan, and in the northeast, Bengal became East Pakistan. The Bengalis shared the Moslem religion with the West Pakistanis, but had little in common culturally and economically. Even their language was different. The two sections were a thousand miles apart in more ways than one.

Jinnah was the first governor-general of the new country and president of its Assembly, but his success was short-lived. He died on September 11, 1948.

CIVIL WAR

Pakistan was created out of bloodshed and conflict. Its birth resulted in the world's largest mass movement of people. Some 7.5 million Moslems from India fled to the two parts of Pakistan, and about 10 million Hindus left Pakistan for the new India. Moslems stopped trains carrying Hindus out of Pakistan and murdered the passengers, and there were similar attacks by Hindus on Moslems fleeing India.

In 1956, a new constitution declared Pakistan an Islamic republic, but there was always an undercurrent of tension between West and East Pakistan. This tension was one of the factors that convinced military leaders they could run the country better than the politicians, and in 1958, the military abolished the Constitution and took control. By 1970, the military had organized elections and seemed prepared to return government

The partition of India and Pakistan resulted in the deaths of over one million people as Hindus and Moslems murdered each other.

to an elected assembly, but events were soon to lead to civil war.

When a cyclone and tidal wave struck East Pakistan in 1970, over 200,000 people were killed. Many Bengalis were convinced that the government in West Pakistan allowed long delays in organizing their relief. Then, because of East Pakistan's numerical superiority, the elections organized by the military resulted in a majority of seats in the new Assembly going to Bengalis. East Pakistan demanded autonomy in all areas of government except foreign policy. When West Pakistan refused to entertain these demands, East Pakistan declared itself an independent nation called Bangladesh in March 1971. West Pakistan then sent the army in to bring Bangladesh under control.

In December 1971, India sided with Bangladesh and went to war against Pakistan. Pakistan was defeated within two weeks, and the war came to an end at the cost of one million lives. Pakistan had lost half its population and a seventh of its area. A new leader of the truncated Pakistan rose to power. His name was Zulfikar Ali Bhutto.

Zulfikar Ali Bhutto, prime minister from 1972 to 1977, was a progressive leader, implementing major reforms to alleviate the plight of the poor.

BHUTTO AND GENERAL ZIA

Bhutto ruled from 1972 to 1977, introducing a new constitution in 1973 based on adult suffrage. For the first time in the country's history, the needs of the poor were addressed and progressive changes were made to the country's educational and health systems. However, Bhutto was also a stern leader who was prepared to send the army into Balochistan when tribal leaders there questioned his authority. Thousands of people died in the Balochistan conflict.

When Bhutto called elections in 1977, widespread allegations of vote-rigging arose and civil disorder erupted across the country. On July 5, 1977, Bhutto was placed under house arrest by General Muhammad Zia ul-Haq. General Zia promised new free elections, but he was still ruling the country when he died in a plane crash in 1988.

In 1977, Zia accused Bhutto of having ordered the murder of a political rival and put him on trial. It is generally agreed that the evidence presented was inconclusive, but Bhutto was found guilty and sentenced to death by hanging. He was executed in 1979.

A modified version of the 1973 Constitution was introduced in 1985, and elections were held under very strict conditions. As a result, they were boycotted by the main opposition groups. The elections in 1988, were a different matter, and this time Benazir Bhutto, the daughter of the executed Bhutto, was elected the new prime minister.

Benazir Bhutto, the first woman to have been prime minister of an Islamic country, did not have the support of the military, and in 1990 she was deposed. New elections were held, but it is generally believed that they were rigged to bring to power someone acceptable to the army. He was Nawaz Sharif. He alienated the army and the president, however, and was deposed by the president in April 1993. A month later, the Supreme Court ruled the ouster illegal, and Nawaz Sharif was reinstated. However, the situation is still tentative, as people wait to see what the army will do.

General Zia ruled Pakistan with an iron fist, and all political opposition was firmly and often violently suppressed. Because Pakistan opposed the Soviet Union's invasion of Afghanistan, international disapproval of Zia's regime was muted by American support for him.

GOVERNMENT

GIVEN PAKISTAN'S TURBULENT HISTORY, it is not surprising that there have been many changes of government. The army continues to be a key player in the process of governing the country. High-ranking members of the armed forces, usually with the support of business interests, have intervened more than once in the government by deposing existing administrations. Nevertheless, a democratic tradition remains, despite the likelihood of vote-rigging and unconstitutional changes enforced by those who gain power.

THE CONSTITUTION

There are two main parties in Pakistan, the Islamic Democratic Alliance headed by Nawaz Sharif, the current prime minister, and the Pakistan People's Party led by Benazir Bhutto. The real power, though, is held by the army and the president.

After East Pakistan became Bangladesh in 1971, it was necessary to reorganize the administration to take account of the new situation. The smaller provinces feared domination by the Punjab, where over 60% of the population lives. Zulfikar Ali Bhutto introduced a constitution that balanced power between a national assembly elected by the whole country and regional assemblies based in Sindh, Punjab, Balochistan, and the North West Frontier Province. Consensus was achieved, and the constitution was formally adopted in 1973. The present Pakistani Constitution is a restricted version of the 1973 Constitution.

The most notably undemocratic feature of the present Constitution arises from an amendment introduced by General Zia in 1985. The amendment gives the unelected president of the country the right to overrule the elected assembly. Pakistan's current president is Ghulam Ishaq Khan, first appointed president in 1988 after General Zia's death.

The 1973 Constitution is the third in Pakistan's history and is likely to remain the basis of any future democracy in the country.

Opposite: **Jinnah Hall in Lahore, the seat of the municipal government.**

In April 1993, the government experienced some upheaval, not an unusual situation for Pakistan. The prime minister, Nawaz Sharif, tried to limit the powers of the president by amending the Constitution, and this provoked the president to depose Sharif. Benazir Bhutto supported the move, provoking much criticism, and she called for new elections. The Supreme Court has since reinstated Nawaz Sharif. Pakistan seems to undergo a political crisis every few years, and this pattern is likely to continue.

BENAZIR BHUTTO

In December 1988, Benazir Bhutto, at 35, became the first woman premier of a modern Islamic state. Despite having been deposed in 1990, she remains enormously popular, especially among the millions of poor peasants who make up the majority of Pakistan's population.

Her upbringing was a very privileged one, as she was born into one of the richest families in Pakistan. She was educated at a series of private English schools in Pakistan, and at the age of 16 went to the United States to study at Harvard-Radcliffe. She then continued her studies at Oxford University in the United Kingdom.

When she returned to Pakistan in 1977, she was expecting to enter the foreign service of a government ruled by her father, Zulfikar Ali Bhutto. But within a week of her return, her father was overthrown by the army and was hanged two years later. Bhutto recalls seeing him for the last time: "The last time I saw him was a few hours before his assassination on April

As president of Pakistan, Ghulam Ishaq Khan has the power to overrule and dismiss the elected Assembly, a power he exercised in 1990, when he deposed Benazir Bhutto, and again in 1993, when he deposed Nawaz Sharif.

Benazir Bhutto

3. He weighed 95 pounds at the time. It was terrible and extremely traumatic. It's a very painful chapter and I don't know how one ever comes to terms with it."

Bhutto was prime minister of Pakistan for two years. In 1991, her husband, labeled a polo-playing millionaire by the press, was arrested and charged with corruption. Bhutto supported her husband's claim of innocence, but he remained in prison without bail for almost two years.

From 1990, Benazir Bhutto maintained pressure on the government of Nawaz Sharif by calling for new elections. In November 1992 her protests reached a climax, and thousands of activists belonging to her party were rounded up and imprisoned. Bhutto herself was banned from leading an anti-government march in Islamabad. Defying the ban, Bhutto appeared in public wearing a bullet-proof vest and swimming goggles for protection against tear gas. She was arrested after a high-speed car chase through the city and banished from the capital for 30 days.

During her years as an opposition leader, Bhutto spent more than five years in prison or under house arrest and was in solitary confinement for a period of 11 months. She always appears in public wearing a bullet-proof vest, escorted by her own security guards.

Bhutto has already played a huge role in Pakistan's government despite being a Moslem woman, and seems determined to continue as a key player in her country's future.

The United Nations has been administering a cease-fire line in the disputed state of Jammu and Kashmir since 1948. Pakistan and India both claim the right to all of the state.

THE PROBLEM OF KASHMIR

When India and Pakistan gained independence, it seemed likely that the province of Kashmir would end up in the new Pakistan. The region has a Moslem majority but was never officially part of British India and so the ruler had to decide whether to join Hindu India or Moslem Pakistan. The Hindu ruler was still undecided when Pakistan invaded, only to be met by the Indian army. Kashmir ended up divided, with approximately two-thirds in India and one-third in Pakistan.

Jammu and Kashmir, as the state is officially known, remains a bone of contention between India and Pakistan. India accuses Pakistan of encouraging and arming the Moslem Kashmiri rebels seeking secession from India. India's reluctance to negotiate with Pakistan on the future of Kashmir is largely motivated by a fear of the likely consequences. India also faces demands for secession from various groups in other parts of the country, and any concession to the Kashmiri separatists would be encouragement for other rebels.

The situation has reached a new crisis since Gorbachev ended the war in Afghanistan in 1989. Weapons that once would have gone from Pakistan to the Afghan *mujahedin* ("moo-JAH-hi-deen"), or rebels, are going instead to Kashmir; the result has been a dramatic and tragic escalation of violence. Pakistan estimates that 25,000 people have died in Kashmir since January 1990.

GOVERNMENT—PATHAN STYLE

Among the hill Pathans, who live in the isolated mountains astride the border with Afghanistan, there is a style of government that has remained unchanged for centuries. In some respects it is anarchic, as there are no written laws and the rule of the national government extends only as far as main roads and a few villages and forts. The central government is represented by a civil servant known as the political agent (PA), who exercises many of the functions of a governor.

The PA does not, however, interfere with the workings of the *jirga* ("jerh-GAH"), the Pathan equivalent of a local council or parliament. The jirga is made up of tribal leaders and, while its decisions are final and irrevocable, there is a strong democratic element in that no one person can control its decision-making processes. Decisions are made on a consensus basis rather than a simple count of hands. Such a procedure reflects the underlying dynamics of the jirga, which is to arrive at a decision that will satisfy and be accepted by all the parties in conflict. Sometimes the jirga will meet to decide on a matter of communal interest like the location of a new mosque.

ECONOMY

PAKISTAN'S ECONOMY is based mainly on agriculture, but there is a basic distinction between the economy of western Pakistan and that of the rest of the country. Ecological factors have encouraged population growth and a sound economy in the fertile areas of Punjab and Sindh, while Balochistan and the North West Frontier Province struggle with subsistence farming.

Historical factors help to explain the slow growth of industry in Pakistan. In 1947, when Pakistan and India emerged as separate nations, there were few factories in the area that is now Pakistan, and the lack of an industrial base has inhibited such development.

Opposite: **Two Punjabi women winnow the harvested wheat. The stalks of wheat are beaten against the ground, and the chaff floats away on the breeze as the heavier wheat falls to the ground.**

Left: Cotton is best picked by hand, which requires a lot of labor. In Pakistan, labor is cheap and plentiful. Workers like these Sindhi peasant women on their way home from the fields are employed to pick the cotton bolls off the shrubs.

Sheep play an important part in the Balochis' struggle for survival. Their fleece is made into clothes and also woven into rugs and sold. They also provide milk and meat.

BALOCHISTAN'S STRUGGLE

The western border regions of Pakistan are the poorest, and the level of economic activity has not changed much over the years. Economically, Balochistan is the least-advanced region of Pakistan. The climate is very dry and does not easily support agriculture. Goats and sheep provide the main source of income, supplemented by a primitive form of agriculture that provides some of the basic necessities. Pastoral nomadism is still practiced in northwest Balochistan, and camels and donkeys often provide the main form of transport for the sparse population. Only a few green valleys in the south support crops mainly of fruit, which is the chief cash crop and is exported to other parts of the country.

Nevertheless, Balochistan possesses an economic potential that could one day benefit its population. There are substantial reserves of coal, sulfur, limestone, and other forms of mineral wealth in the region. Natural gas was first exploited here in the early 1950s, and Balochistan now produces almost 50% of the country's electric power.

THE NORTH WEST FRONTIER PROVINCE

Northwest Pakistan does not have the benefit of any wealth-creating resources and is heavily dependent upon agriculture for its economic survival. Four out of five people here are employed in agriculture. Wheat, sugarcane, and tobacco are the principal crops. The few industries that do exist are agricultural spin-offs, like sugar-refining, fruit-canning, and tobacco-processing.

When this region was under British control, it was considered to be of major strategic importance because of its proximity to Afghanistan and Russia. Consequently, a number of road and rail networks were laid down to facilitate military communication and the transport of troops. This existing infrastructure has benefited the region's agriculture-related industries.

Two peasants carry harvested sheaves of wheat away from the fields in preparation for winnowing. Pakistani peasants have never heard of a combine, and farm labor is done without the aid of machinery.

Sugarcane is an important crop in both Punjab and Sindh, which are blessed with fertile alluvial soil deposited by the mighty Indus.

PUNJAB AND SINDH

The Indus River has not only provided rich alluvial soils, but has also facilitated extensive irrigation that now reaches what were once vast sandy tracts of desert. Today, some three-quarters of Punjab's cultivated land is irrigated. Wheat, millet, rice, and sugarcane are some of the most profitable crops. Mangoes, guavas, and citrus fruits are the main fruit crops.

Sindh's economy is also mainly agricultural, with the same kind of crops and fruits grown as in Punjab. Sindh has 150 miles of coastline, with backwaters that spread inland in all directions for hundreds of square miles. This provides a rich source for marine fishing.

Unlike the western regions of Pakistan, both Punjab and Sindh have important industrial areas. Punjab has highly industrialized areas producing machines and electrical appliances. It is also the region that produces many of the millions of bicycles and rickshaws used throughout the country.

Sindh's most important industrial activity concerns cotton. The province produces one-third of the country's cotton output. Almost half of Pakistan's cotton textile mills are located in this region. The growing and harvesting of cotton, also found in the Punjab, plays a crucial role in the country's economy. Other heavy industries in Sindh include cement production, steelworks, and a car factory in Karachi. There are also many light industrial centers, some of which are built around workshops where artisans produce handicrafts.

COTTON

Cotton is a shrub which reaches an average height of about six feet and needs a warm climate for germination and growth, followed by dry conditions for harvesting. The weather in Punjab and Sindh is ideal in this respect, and Pakistan is also able to provide the large amount of human labor necessary for cotton harvesting. Mechanical harvesters are used in the United States, but in Pakistan it is far more common to see people picking by hand the fruit capsules, known as bolls, which contain the mass of white fibers that becomes cotton.

Before 1947, the area of British India that is now Pakistan only supplied raw cotton to other parts of the colony for processing and manufacturing. During the 1950s, however, there was a rapid expansion in the cotton-textile and cotton-yarn industries, and Pakistan now exports both cotton yarn and cloth, as well as the raw material. Indeed, cotton-textile mills account for a large proportion of the total industrial labor force in Pakistan today.

MONEY FROM ABROAD

It has been estimated that Pakistan earns its largest amount of foreign currency not through the export of some valuable commodity, but by means of its own people returning home with money earned abroad. Over 1.5 million Pakistanis work abroad as general workers as well as skilled technicians and professionals, especially in the oil-rich Middle Eastern countries.

Large communities of Pakistanis live in the United States and the United Kingdom. Although permanently settled in these countries, they regularly send money to their families in Pakistan.

AN ISLAMIC ECONOMY?

After 1977, when General Zia imposed martial rule, a process of Islamization was begun that extended to economic aspects of life. An Islamic Ideology Council was created with the responsibility of ensuring that the laws of the country were brought in line with the fundamental principles of the state religion. Among other matters, this involved making mandatory the *zakat* ("zeh-KAHT")—a tax on various types of personal income—and the *ushr* ("OOSH-rerh"), a similar tax on land.

Moslem theology forbids the levying of interest on loans, and the Islamic Ideology Council was faced with the task of squaring this prohibition with one of the basic facts of life for any modern capitalist state. Proposals have been made to set up banks and other financial institutions that do not function using *riba* ("ri-BAH"), or interest, but there is also an unwillingness on the part of many of Pakistan's leaders to interfere too much with the conventional dynamics of the free-market economy. It remains unclear just how far the country's economy will go to adjust to the strict demands of Islam.

ECONOMIC FACTS

- Seventy percent of Pakistanis are employed in agriculture.
- Ten percent are employed in manufacturing industries.
- China, Japan, the United Kingdom, the United States, and Germany are Pakistan's main trading partners.
- Imports: Chemicals, iron and steel, petroleum products, electrical equipment
- Exports: Cotton, carpets, leather goods, wool

Opposite: **Pakistani banks, like the Habib Bank in Karachi, are trying to juggle the demands of the modern financial world and the strictures of Islam.**

PAKISTANIS

THERE ARE FIVE MAJOR GROUPS of people in Pakistan; four of them are named after the regions they predominantly inhabit. However, such a neat summary cannot do justice to the complexity of race in Pakistan. Successive waves of migration have brought an astonishing array of people into the country: Persians, Greeks, Moghuls, Indians, Arabs, and a host of other Middle Eastern races have, over the centuries, complicated the racial mixture of the country's population. Differences between the major groups are sometimes dramatic and manifest themselves in physical features as well as dress and language. Despite this, there is a unifying sense of being Pakistani, which comes in part from a common religion that helps define a shared set of values.

Opposite: **A young Kalash girl. "Kalash" comes from** *"kala,"* **meaning "black" in Urdu. They are called the black people because of the black clothes the women and girls wear.**

Below: **A group of schoolboys from the northern Chitral Valley. Schools are segregated: boys are taught by male teachers and girls by female teachers.**

A tribal Sindhi woman takes a break from her work to sit and meditate.

Opposite: **A young Sindhi man wearing the traditional embroidered cap and ajrak. The ajraks are like the Scottish tartans—each tribe or clan has its own distinctive pattern and the male members wear their colors with pride.**

THE SINDHIS

Sindh is noteworthy for being the area of Pakistan with the largest number of Hindus. The whole province was Hindu before its rulers were overthrown by Moslems. Today, despite the majority of its inhabitants being Moslems, certain Hindu customs, like the putting of palms together in greeting, still persist.

It is only recently that Sindh has developed its agricultural potential, due to the extensive network of canals that has been laid down. There is still a tradition of hunting for food, and many of the poorer Hindus still maintain a precarious existence in this way by living off the riverine jungle land. In many of the small towns that have grown up along the rivers, there are families who trace their origins to Turkey and Afghanistan. Many place names are simply called "Shah," betraying their common Arab ancestry.

Elsewhere, wealthy landlords hold enormous social and political power and peasants live a semi-feudal existence. It is not uncommon to find peasants suffering under a medieval type of servitude, being obliged to give as much as 80% of their harvest to landlords. Ironically, modern agricultural innovations, like mechanization and irrigation schemes, are worsening the peasants' plight. The new methods force many small farmers off the plots of land their families worked for generations. Landlords make more profit by cultivating larger areas of land, obtained by buying off numerous small landholders. In many ways the situation is similar to the plight of American farmers described in John Steinbeck's *The Grapes of Wrath*.

The distinctive feature of male dress in Sindh is the *ajrak* ("aj-RAHK"), a red cloth, about six and a half feet long and 24–36 inches wide, which is worn over the shoulder of the *kurta hizar* ("KOOR-tah i-ZAHR"), the long shirt and baggy pants worn by men. Individual tribes weave their unique pattern into the ajrak, which is hand-dyed using vegetable dyes and cow dung. Another highly colorful item of dress is the embroidered cloth cap with tiny mirrors stitched into it. Women, who do not wear the colorful caps, make up for it by embroidering their shirt-fronts with bright color schemes of their own.

This young girl is of typical Punjabi stock—well-built and fair-skinned.

THE PUNJABIS

With approximately 75 million people living in the "land of the five rivers," Punjabis make up over 60% of the country's population. This numerical superiority, along with their living in the most fertile and prosperous region of Pakistan, explains the fact that Punjabis constitute a large proportion of the country's political and social elite. Punjabis also figure prominently among the leading military figures who play an important role in the government of the country.

Most farmers in the central parts of the Punjab own their land. The situation is very different from the region's southwest parts, and Sindh generally, where aristocratic land-owning families still dominate and peasants have to give a percentage of their harvest to their landlords as payment for cultivating the land.

Punjabi traditional dress is characterized for males by the wearing of a shirt over a long cloth wrap known as a *dhoti* ("DHOH-ti"). On the head a turban is normally worn, except in informal situations. Female Punjabi dress is not distinctively different from that of Pakistani women generally, namely the wide trousers and long shirt known as the *shalwar kamiz* ("shehl-WAHR kha-MEEZ"), with a *dupatta* ("doo-PEHT-tah"), a veil. Punjabis are usually well-built, tall, and fair-complexioned compared to Pakistanis of other regions.

THE MOHAJIRS

Mohajir ("mo-HAH-jir"), meaning "refugee," is the name given to the Moslems who arrived in Pakistan at the time of partition from India. In 1947, Mohajir families loaded their belongings and either took a train or walked across the border to Pakistan, braving violence along the way. Many left India because they owned small businesses and felt that their livelihoods would be threatened in a predominantly Hindu state. Being commercially minded, the majority of them settled in Karachi, the country's industrial center, and re-established their enterprises in the form of family businesses there. Many Mohajirs also settled in the other large cities of Pakistan: Islamabad, Rawalpindi, and Hyderabad. To some extent they still see themselves, and are sometimes viewed by other Pakistanis, as outsiders. Around Karachi they have grouped themselves into a fairly close-knit community.

Two factors emphasize their difference from the majority of Pakistanis. Although the Mohajirs came from different parts of India, a unifying factor among them was their native Urdu language. Most Pakistanis, however, have to learn their national language at school. Another factor that has helped cause anti-Mohajir resentment also goes back to the days of Partition. As the Mohajirs were arriving in Karachi, thousands of Hindus, who had formerly made up a minority in the city, were fleeing across the new border to India. The city jobs they left behind, many of them commercially important positions, tended to be filled by the enterprising Mohajirs. Over the years, natives of Sindh have benefited from educational opportunities and now feel that they, not the "outsiders," should hold these positions of responsibility and influence. At its worst, resentment against the Mohajirs has expressed itself in acts of violence.

Mohajirs suffered greatly during the upheaval of Partition, and as a result have grouped themselves into a community that wields enormous social and political influence.

Pathans claim Aryan descent, but many scholars believe they are in fact the lost tribe of Israel.

THE PATHANS

The Pathans live in the North West Frontier Province and, while there are many Pathan tribes, a basic division can be made between those who live and work as settled peasants and those who inhabit the mountains that straddle the border with Afghanistan. These mountain-dwelling Pathans have a justified reputation for being a warlike and rugged people. Their social environment bears some resemblance to the early days of America's Wild West in that the carrying of guns and knives is considered normal and expected behavior.

In keeping with their warlike reputation, Pathans tend to be tall and strongly built with a high regard for fighting prowess. In the 19th century, they were the scourge of the British, who fought numerous unsuccessful battles against them, attempting to secure control of the Khyber Pass. The British dubbed them the best guerrilla fighters in Asia.

The Pathan tribes are fiercely insular and conservative, and in some respects they live on the periphery of mainstream Pakistani life. Conflict with government agencies is common, and when, for example, plans were made for a new road to be built across the land belonging to one tribe, resistance by the Pathans escalated into pitched battles with the authorities. The issue has still not been settled!

The total Pathan population is estimated at between 15 million and 17 million, with 10 million living in Pakistan and the rest in Afghanistan.

THE KALASH OF THE HINDU KUSH

The Kalash people are small in number, hardly exceeding 3,000, but they distinguish themselves from most other Pakistanis in a number of interesting ways. They live among the northern mountains of the Hindu Kush, and as well as having their own language and costume, they practice animism (the worship of spirits in nature), which is quite removed from Islam, its origin unknown. Like many minority cultures around the world, their way of life is increasingly under threat as the outside world impinges more and more on what was a unique lifestyle.

Festivals, weddings, and funerals are occasions for flamboyant displays of music and dance where the women, who are never kept in seclusion, take to the dancing ground and perform traditional dances that have always excluded men. In their normal dress, Kalash women have a highly distinctive costume characterized by the generous use of cowrie shells. The shells decorate a train that hangs down from the back of the head to well below the shoulders. The embroidered train is covered with rows of the shells, interspersed with colored beads and coin-shaped pieces of metal, with the different shapes and sizes of the shells creating patterns that go across, up, and down the train.

In other respects, the role of Kalash women is highly circumscribed. Kalash villages have an area where women are forbidden to enter and partake in the religious ceremonies conducted there by the men. The beehive is seen as a paradigm of an all-male world, and consequently the eating of honey by women is also forbidden. Women do have rights of their own, however. The idea of a broken marriage is acknowledged, and a woman can leave her husband, discuss the terms of a divorce, and remarry.

THE BALOCHIS

The Balochis of Balochistan are ethnically related to the Pathans and it is difficult to observe any significant difference in their features. Like the Pathans, the Balochis are fiercely independent, and they have proved just as resistant to change and bureaucratic control. Unlike the Pathans, however, they are semi-nomadic, and some clans have drifted into Sindh and taken up life as peasants. The Balochis who retain a nomadic way of life are driven by the need to find fresh grass for their herds of sheep and goats and to avoid the punishing extremes of temperature. If lucky, a Balochi family will have its own horse. Donkeys and camels are kept for their usefulness in transporting goods.

The exact origin of the Balochis is a matter of some dispute. The notion that, like the Pathans, they descend from one of the 10 Lost Tribes of Israel is as unlikely to be true as another theory that traces their roots back to Babylon. The latter theory is largely based on the similarity between Baloch and Baal, the Babylonian god, and Belos, one of the Babylonian rulers. It is more likely that they originate from the Caspian Sea region and traveled across Iran to reach present-day Balochistan some time around A.D. 1000.

The Balochis resemble the Pathans, but they are more likely to wear their hair and beards long. They have an aversion to egg-shaped skulls, and mothers will bandage and stroke their babies' heads in an attempt to mold a more rounded appearance. Distinctive features of Balochi dress include a preference for white, suited to the arid and hot climate, and very large turbans, known as *pag* ("PAHG"), which use up to 6 feet of cloth. Their baggy trousers, which require an even more generous length of cloth, use twice as much material as their turbans, and are worn under long robes.

In recent years the Balochis have been adversely affected by economic developments that might have been expected to benefit them. Natural gas fields have been discovered, along with coal, sulfur, and significant sources of various valuable minerals. The result has been a sudden surge of immigration from other regions of the country, and the native Balochis have not reaped any great advantage. Quite the contrary, for road-building and immigration have only served to disrupt their traditional way of life. A further bone of contention was the development of grazing lands in the east of Balochistan into cultivated fields fed by newly built irrigation canals. This too attracted new settlers, and in 1970 there was a violent uprising among some Balochi tribes. This was eventually suppressed by the army, only to be followed by the Soviet invasion of Afghanistan, which resulted in thousands of new refugees. The Balochis are now in danger of becoming a minority in their own land.

Like the Pathan jirga (see page 31), Balochi tribes hold a council of leaders to discuss and decide on matters of importance to the community.

LIFESTYLE

FAMILY LIFE IN PAKISTAN is firmly patriarchal and based around the extended family, with three, even four generations living together. Wage-earning members of a family accept the obligation to care for those too old or too young to manage by themselves. There is a strong sense of family solidarity. Respect is always accorded to those older in years, and children are taught to obey their fathers and to go on obeying them even when they themselves are grown up and have children of their own.

While children are brought up strictly in terms of obeying their elders, in other ways they are pampered. There are few family events to which young children are not invited, and their noisy presence at a party is always tolerated, even late at night. Young boys are particularly spoiled and receive preferential treatment. They are not expected to run as many errands as their sisters, and their misbehavior is tolerated where that of their sisters would earn a reprimand. Generally, children are introduced early to role patterns that will shape their adult behavior and attitudes.

The husband in a family is not likely to share in daily household duties. He will leave for work each day and return in the evening expecting his meal to be ready. This is accepted by everyone in the family and neighborhood as normal. When he has free time, he is most likely to spend it outside his home in the company of male friends. His wife is viewed as the family's daughter-in-law, and her household duties extend to her husband's family as a whole. In Pakistan's modern cities, however, the traditional pattern of family life is beginning to change. It is no longer unheard of for a young couple to wish to live alone, and more would probably do so if financially secure enough.

Opposite: **While the men are out gathering berries or making pots, these tribal Sindhi women contribute to their family's livelihood by sewing patchwork quilts that will be sold in a market town.**

Above: **In a typical city-dwelling Pakistani family, the older women have their hair covered by a dupatta, while the young women wear their hair short and uncovered.**

THE POSITION OF WOMEN

Women are not seen as independent wage-earners, which explains the traditional preference for boys over girls. The birth of a son represents a potential source of income and an additional provision for old age. A baby girl, however, will eventually marry and leave. A woman who does not marry remains a constant burden on the family's income. It is difficult, then, for a woman to shrug off the shame of not being married.

The inferior status of women is represented at its most extreme by the practice of purdah ("PERH-dah"). A woman "in purdah" lives a form of apartheid that involves almost complete segregation from the male world. She is never seen in the company of men except for her husband and close relatives. She never leaves her house unaccompanied, and always wears the *burquah* ("berh-KWAH"), a full-length cover over the body and face.

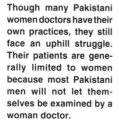

Though many Pakistani women doctors have their own practices, they still face an uphill struggle. Their patients are generally limited to women because most Pakistani men will not let themselves be examined by a woman doctor.

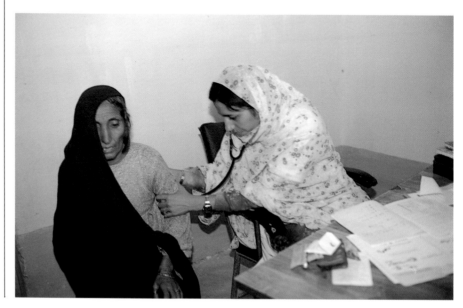

The perceived inferiority of women is deeply rooted in the Pakistani psyche. It reveals itself in the educational system, especially in rural areas, where only 10% of the female population attends school. Even in towns and cities the proportion of girls to boys in secondary education is dramatically low. Schooling is not seen as necessary for girls because employment that requires formal education is regarded as suitable only for males. There is also a feeling that "too much" education will only unsettle a girl by creating aspirations that cannot be fulfilled, as well as make her less attractive as a marriage partner.

The position of women in Pakistan is, however, very complex. A woman was elected prime minister in 1988. Also, Pakistan was one of the first countries to appoint women ambassadors. When it comes to skilled professions, women compete equally with men. Pakistan International Airlines, for instance, employs more female pilots than any other airline in the world. Women in purdah are more likely to come from the urban, middle-class families because it is seen as a good reflection of the family's social status if the women do not need to work.

Ayesha Rabia Naveed is Pakistan International Airlines' (PIA) first woman jet pilot.

THE BURQUAH

There are two types of burquah. One is made from black material and is a cloak-like, long-sleeved coat with a separate piece of cloth that covers the head and shoulders. The face is shrouded by three thin veils that are sewn onto the top of the black headscarf. Sometimes the veils are arranged so that only the top part of the face is visible, and sometimes two of the veils can be thrown back over the shoulder. This type of burquah is commonly worn by women from middle-class families and is considered quite fashionable.

The other type of burquah is more common in small towns and rural villages. It is white and also consists of two parts: a main shroud for the body made up of thick cotton, and a separate, tightly fitting headpiece. The face is covered by close-fitted netting that allows the wearer to see through it.

Both types of burquah are impractical for most work situations. Women arriving at an office or factory remove the burquah and just wear the thin veil known as the *dupatta* around their head and shoulders, or as a loose scarf. In rural areas where women work hard in the fields, the burquah is reserved for occasions when they go out shopping, for instance. In the Punjab, the picking of cotton is exclusively women's work and wearing the burquah for this type of labor would be highly impractical.

The burquah is more of a lifestyle signifier than an item of national dress. Differences in style, especially regarding the amount of the face that is visible, have more to do with social class and a woman's view of herself than anything else. In urban, middle-class areas, the burquah is regarded as old-fashioned, and some emancipated women have their hair cut short and wear no dupatta or scarf. More traditionally minded people would regard the absence of any head garment as quite shocking, and Benazir Bhutto, for instance, is never seen in public without some kind of scarf worn over her head.

A rural Balochi father carrying his son during a procession to celebrate the boy's circumcision.

CIRCUMCISION

Apart from his wedding day, this is the most important event in the life of a Pakistani male. But as it usually happens between the ages of two and five, he is unlikely to recognize its significance at the time. Only among the poorer and more traditionally minded people is the event likely to take place at a later age. Most families arrange for the circumcision to take place in the hospital before the newborn leaves. In rural areas there is always someone, often the local barber, who is experienced at performing the procedure (without anesthesia), and he is called upon whenever necessary.

The act of circumcision is a religious requirement for male Moslems, and the event is celebrated by a feast. Better-educated, urban families are likely to arrange a party at home for members of the family and close friends. In the countryside, by tradition, the whole family as well as neighbors and friends attend the feast that takes place after the circumcision. The child will be dressed in his best set of clothes and will receive small gifts of money from the guests.

A rural man, dressed in his best clothes and the traditional veil, on the way to his wedding where he may meet his future wife for the first time.

MARRIAGE

Marriage is less a social and emotional bonding between two individuals and more a tie between different families and a source of prestige for everyone involved. Arranged marriages are taken for granted and the bride and groom may often be surprised at the choice made for them by their parents. In some parts of the country, a marriage is arranged even before the couple is born, nor is it unheard of for a couple to see each other for the first time only on the day of the wedding. In urban areas, however, this is now regarded as old-fashioned and undesirable. Instead, once an engagement has been formally announced, the couple may start to go out together, usually accompanied by a chaperone such as the girl's sister. The agreement of the couple is looked for before any formal arrangement is made, and if there were strong objections by either party, many parents would try to respect their child's wishes. Young people are brought up, though, to think of love as something that develops within a marriage, not as a precondition for it. In rural areas a woman is expected to marry before she is 20; in cities, a few years later.

The dowry is an essential part of a wedding. Traditionally, it consisted of gifts of jewelry and clothes, but nowadays items like refrigerators and television sets are just as likely to be featured. The higher the family is on the social scale, the more valuable and prestigious the dowry becomes, but for all parents it is financially the most demanding time of their lives. Usually it is up to the bride's parents to provide the dowry, but in some tribes the groom's parents present the dowry to the bride's family. The cost of the wedding party itself, often involving hundreds of guests, is always borne by the bride's parents.

For two weeks before the wedding, the bride will remain inside her house while her family and friends prepare for the big event. Before the actual wedding day, the most important event is the *mehndi* ("muh-HEN-di") ceremony. "Mehndi" means "henna," a plant that produces a dye used for coloring the hands and feet. The henna is symbolically applied to the hands of the bride by the groom's sister or mother. Afterward the henna is washed off and then reapplied by

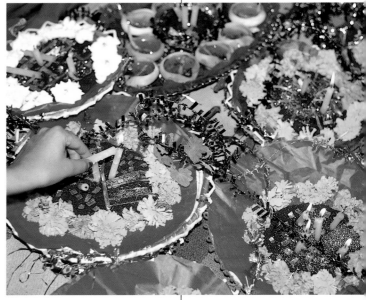

The wedding party is always hosted by the bride's family, and the beautiful decoration of the food is a matter of pride.

someone who is able to expertly create elaborate floral designs on the hands and feet. The importance of the mehndi ceremony derives from the formal coming together of the two families and always unfolds in two stages. First the bride will stay at home while her family visits the groom's house, and then, the next day, the groom remains indoors while his family visits the bride's house where the mehndi ceremony takes place.

The wedding itself is a sumptuous affair characterized by a lavish party, often held a few days after the civil formalities in which papers are signed specifying the dowry and other matters. The newlyweds remain formally seated throughout the festivities and eat separately from the main body of guests. At some point in the evening, the couple will ceremonially depart for·the groom's house, traditionally in a palanquin (a covered couch) on a horse or camel, but nowadays it is just as likely to be in a decorated car.

DEATH

Relatives and friends arrive at the home of the deceased as soon as possible after receiving the news. They wait outside the house until close relatives have paid their last respects and then enter to recite some prayers by the side of the corpse, which is then wrapped in a white shroud, sprinkled with rose petals, and taken to be buried.

Women do not accompany the body to the burial ground. Men carry the body on a stretcher, or, in the case of a young child, the father carries the body in his arms. At the cemetery, the final prayers for the repose of the deceased are said. Moslems are not buried in coffins; a plank is placed at the bottom of the grave and the body is laid on top of that. The face is covered before the body is lowered into the ground. Male relatives sprinkle the grave with earth before it is completely filled in.

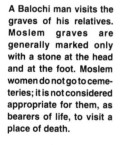

A Balochi man visits the graves of his relatives. Moslem graves are generally marked only with a stone at the head and at the foot. Moslem women do not go to cemeteries; it is not considered appropriate for them, as bearers of life, to visit a place of death.

HOSPITALITY

The family is at the heart of Pakistani life. Public life in Pakistan is in many ways impersonal and cold, but this is partly because citizens reserve their warmth and sociability for the confines of their own homes. This does not breed selfishness and insularity, however, for the concept of the guest plays an important role in the family. Any family that can afford the expense will have a special guest room where visitors are invited to spend time with the family. Such a special room is a rather grand manifestation of the need to acknowledge the importance of showing hospitality to a guest. The same respect for a visitor is found among the poorest of families.

The giving of small gifts to a guest is a common observance among Pakistani families of all regions and classes. It may only be a piece of cloth, but it represents the tremendous respect that is accorded any visitor to a Pakistani home.

Among the tribal Pathans, showing hospitality to visitors is one of the cornerstones of their social code. In a house built of mud and stone, even a tribal leader himself will stir the milk in a visitor's tea and add the sugar as a mark of his humility in welcoming someone into his home. Each Pathan village will usually have a house with dormitory beds built for the sole purpose of accommodating guests.

THE PATHAN CODE OF HONOR

Honor is central to the Pakistani value system, and among the Pathans it is practiced with a zeal and commitment that sets them apart. Their code for living is called *Pukhtunwali* ("PUHK-tuhn-wah-lee"), and the notion of acting honorably is its basic tenet. This involves avenging any insult against self, family, or tribe. Although not inscribed in any statute, it has the same force as a law and is expressed in the proverb: "He is not a Pathan who does not give a blow for a pinch."

There is a fierce regard for what is considered a woman's rightful role. Any deviation from a strict set of unwritten rules is liable to meet a severe punishment. A case of adultery, for instance, could easily result in the man being swiftly executed and the woman summarily divorced and handed over to the dead man's family, where she is treated like a slave and worked into an early grave.

Opposite: It is a rare sight to see a Pathan without a gun or rifle. An American journalist once asked an armed Pathan whether it was really necessary to carry a loaded pistol. "Why do you Americans have the atomic bomb?" the Pathan asked in response. "Is it not to keep peace in the world? I carry a gun so no one will bother me."

Sometimes an honor dispute will continue from one generation to the next. Whole families have been wiped out in this manner. The need for the aggrieved party to achieve satisfaction takes primacy over the need to punish the aggressor.

Another feature of the Pathan lifestyle is the concept of *melmastia* ("mel-MAHS-tyah"), similar to the concept of sanctuary, which insists that anyone asking for protection should receive it unconditionally. This means that a criminal, arriving in a Pathan village, can claim sanctuary from the police. Sometimes an entire village will take up arms to protect a stranger who has claimed sanctuary.

The concept of honor is so important that Pathans use it, instead of racial origins or a common language, as a definition of their own identity. One is considered a Pathan if one adheres to *Pukhtunwali;* one who shows a wanton disregard for the honor code is not.

THE RICH AND THE POOR

The lowest social class is made up of people who earn their living as cleaners. The work of a paid cleaner, either for a private house or the public streets, is considered beneath the dignity of a Pakistani Moslem, even a very poor one. It is usually Christians, and sometimes Hindus, who do the job. There is no caste system in Pakistan, but the country does have its untouchables—social outcasts shunned by society at large—and these are the cleaners.

The cleaners are careful not to touch anyone; to do so would be considered outrageous. Sometimes they go about their work with their faces covered by a shroud that only allows them to see out in order not to be recognized, for being a cleaner is something to be ashamed of. No one would willingly marry a cleaner except another cleaner, and as a

Cleaners generally live in the slums of the city.

group they tend to live in the poorest part of any town. Their wages are the lowest possible; this is reflected in the ghettos where they live. The only time they receive some acknowledgment is at Christmas, when they sing carols outside the houses they clean and receive a small cash bonus.

At the other end of the social spectrum are the millionaires and near-millionaires. Their wealth often derives from the vast tracts of farming lands they own. The Bhutto family is one example of this class. During the 1960s, 22 aristocratic families controlled nearly all of Pakistan's wealth. Since then, new wealth has been created by owners of large and successful businesses in the major cities.

The lifestyle of the very rich has little in common with the rest of the population. Children of such families go to private, English schools, often completing their education in private boarding schools or prestigious universities in the United Kingdom or the United States. Their acquisition of Western values extends to styles of dress, another factor that separates them from the ordinary citizens.

RELIGION

RELIGION is the fundamental reason for the existence of Pakistan, so it is not surprising that it plays a large part in the life of nearly every citizen. The country was established as an Islamic state in 1947, and millions of Moslems left their homes in India and made their way to the new country. There are a few non-Moslem minorities and they have the right to religious freedom.

ISLAM

Mohammed began preaching Islam in Mecca around A.D. 610. This enraged the town and he was expelled. The flight of Mohammed from Mecca to Medina is called the *Hegira* ("HIJ-rah") and the Moslem calendar is dated from that year, 622. Eight years later, Mohammed and his followers

Opposite: **All Moslem children are taught to recite the Koran in the original Arabic at a young age.**

Left: **The entrance to the Badshahi Masjid, the second-largest mosque in Pakistan, built in 1674 by the Moghul emperor Aurangzeb.**

At the prescribed times, devout Moslems will stop to say their prayers, no matter if they are at a friend's house or in the middle of the Thal Desert.

returned to Mecca and occupied the city in the name of Islam. Since then, Mecca and Medina have been sacred cities of Islam, and every devout Moslem hopes one day to be able to visit Mecca.

Islam spread outward from Mecca to the east and west. In 711, a Moslem Arab general conquered Sindh. He brought with him the revelations of Mohammed that had been memorized and written down into a holy book, the Koran. Moslems believe that the Koran is the word of *Allah* (which means "God" in Arabic) himself, revealed to Mohammed by an angel. The Koran spells out the primary and absolute unity of Allah, who sends out prophets with sacred books designed to educate people about their duties to Allah and to each other. Mohammed is the last prophet, having been preceded by Jesus and the prophets of the Old Testament.

Islam and Christianity share many beliefs and customs. Both stress the importance of compassion for the poor, and in Islam the giving of alms to the poor is one of the five "Pillars of Faith." Moslems are obliged to give 2.5% of their income to those in need, and in Pakistan this is deducted by

THE FIVE PILLARS OF FAITH

- Belief in the oneness of Allah and the prophethood of Mohammed
- Five daily prayers
- The giving of alms to the needy
- Fasting during the month of Ramazan
- Pilgrimage to Mecca

law from bank accounts. Both Islam and Christianity posit the notion that life on earth is a preparation for the next and share the idea that one's behavior on earth will determine the course of life after death. According to Islam, on Judgment Day, the record of a person's life will be presented. If the record book is placed in the right hand, indicating that a good life was lived, a place in heaven is secured. If placed in the left hand, the person is condemned to eternal punishment in hell.

In Islam, representation of human or animal figures is prohibited. Other taboos include gambling, eating pork, and drinking alcohol. Charging interest for the lending of money is also forbidden. This is a problem for a modern Islamic state like Pakistan. In December 1991, the Federal Shariat Court, set up to review the country's laws in the light of Islam's teachings, confirmed that charging interest is illegal. The court recommended that all financial laws be amended to conform with this, and 20 different laws concerning land acquisition, moneylending, and insurance were affected. One of Pakistan's privatized banks has appealed the decision to the country's Supreme Court.

The ruling of the Federal Shariat Court is just one example of the work of the Council of Islamic Ideology, established in 1984. The council has the difficult task of arriving at interpretations of Islamic law that will be acceptable to the more than 70 Moslem sects in Pakistan. Since there had been no organization to set down a unified set of laws before 1947, slightly varying interpretations had evolved among the different sects.

Many children are sent to the mosque after school for religious lessons that include learning to recite from the Koran.

ISLAMIC CUSTOMS

Devout Pakistanis, like Moslems everywhere, pray five times daily facing Mecca. The exact times—sunrise, noon, afternoon, sunset, and night—are announced from the minaret, the tower of a mosque. Nowadays this is likely to be an electronic recording relayed through loudspeakers, but by tradition the announcer is a crier known as the *muezzin* ("moo-EZ-zin"). The announcement, called the *Azan* (a-ZAHN), takes the form of the declaration of the first Pillar of Faith: "In the name of Allah, the Almighty, the Merciful ... There is no god but Allah and Mohammad is his messenger."

Friday is the special prayer day throughout the Moslem world, and most male Pakistanis try to visit a mosque for noon prayers on that day. Before praying on a clean mat, there is a ceremonial washing of the face, hands, and feet. The prayer leader, the imam, faces Mecca and the worshipers stand behind him. Most mosques are not open for prayers to women, but if they are, the women will stand behind the men and join in the recitation of passages from the Koran. Ritualistic movements take the form of bowing from the hips and kneeling with the face to the ground.

Most women conduct their prayers in the privacy of their bedrooms, also on a mat and facing Mecca. Any visitor to Pakistan who stays in a hotel will discover a small arrow, positioned on the ceiling of the room, indicating the direction of Mecca as an aid for prayers conducted in the room.

Every Pakistani man and woman hopes one day to be able to make a pilgrimage to Mecca. Such a visit, called *Haj* ("HAHJ"), is actually commanded in the Koran, and every year well over 50,000 pilgrims depart from Pakistan on organized trips. The visit usually takes place over a short, two-week period during the 12th month of the Islamic calendar. In Mecca, the most important ceremony involves walking around the Ka'bah ("KAH-bah") seven times and kissing the sacred black stone, a meteorite set into the east corner of its wall. The Ka'bah is a small cube-shaped building inside the Great Mosque. Its sacredness derives from the fact that it was here that Mohammed stripped the site of its former pagan idols and established it as the spiritual center of Islam.

After returning from Mecca a male pilgrim adopts the title "Haji" and is addressed as such in public. Women earn the title "Hajiani," but it is not used as a form of address.

Opposite: **The muezzin announces the *Azan*, calling the faithful to prayer.**

Above: **This elderly man is finally realizing a dream he has been planning and saving for most of his life—going on *Haj* to Mecca.**

SHRINES

Shrines are frequently visited by Pakistanis searching for spiritual guidance as well as material help. Women who are threatened with divorce because they have not given birth to a boy, for instance, will repeatedly visit a shrine and pray devotedly in the hope that their wish will be fulfilled. Padlocks will sometimes be fastened to the grille of a shrine and opened only after the devotee's wish has been granted.

Shrines are built around the tombs of saintly individuals and are often elaborately decorated by grateful worshipers. The tomb itself will be festooned with flowers, and the surrounding shrine building will be decorated with small mirrors and other embellishments. Hundreds of people will gather at shrines, usually on a Thursday evening, to listen to the chanting of religious songs. All the saints have their own festivals—called *urs* ("OORS")—when thousands of devotees converge on a particular shrine to celebrate the anniversary of the saint's death. Special buses bring in worshipers from distant localities and others trek for miles across deserts to be present at such an occasion.

One of the most important shrines is the mausoleum of Sheikh Osman of Marwand, known as Shah Lal Baz Qalandar. Osman arrived in Pakistan in 1260 from his native Iran, and when he died in 1274 his tomb quickly became a shrine, being added to and embellished over the centuries. Today, the mausoleum is a large building covered with blue glazed tiles and silver spires on the domes. Outside the shrine Moslem *fakirs* ("feh-KEERS") take up the yogic position and calmly meditate as hundreds of other devotees pass by on their way to visit the shrine. Annually, on the anniversary of Osman's death, the shrine is the focus for a festival attended by people from all over the country.

The shrine of Rukh-e-Alam in Multan.

Another important shrine is Bhit Shah ("the Mound of the King"), 31 miles north of Hyderabad, commemorating a rich man by the name of Shah Abdul Latif who gave up his wealth to embrace the poor and the needy. His religious songs express sentiments that seem close to those of Christianity:

Arise! You have no voice,
God hearkens to the meek.
Sing and play music for your Lord ...

What does the Lord care for name and pedigree,
he favors those skilful in their trade.

A Shiite man reading the Koran in a mosque. Shiites are a minority in the Islamic world.

MOSLEM SECTS

Most Moslem sects fall under the two major groupings of Sunnis and Shiites. These two groups originated in a seventh-century split in Islam when a successor to Mohammed was killed. Ali, Mohammed's son-in-law, then took over the leadership position. Ali was assassinated in 661 by the governor of Syria, who set himself up as the leader, or caliph, in preference to the descendants of Ali. Shiites believe Ali and his descendants to be the true leaders of the faith, having a divine right that is traced back to the seventh-century events. Shiites constitute a minority in the Moslem ranks, however, both in Pakistan and the world at large. The majority of Moslems are Sunnis, who believe that Ali was only one of the caliphs destined to lead the religion in accordance with the *Sunna* ("SOON-nah")—the example of the Prophet.

Sunnis and Shiites share many religious beliefs, although Shiites have their own clerics and tend to worship in their own mosques whenever possible. Shiites commemorate Muharram, the anniversary of the martyring of Mohammad's grandson Hussein, in a more dramatic manner than Sunnis.

The adherents of a Moslem sect founded in the 19th century, known as the Ahmadis, claim to be the rightful successors to Mohammed. Because of the close link between politics and religion in Pakistan, the government declared the sect a minority in 1974. To the outsider, however, they are just another Moslem sect that follows the Koran as religiously as the mainstream.

THE IMAM AND THE CLERIC

An imam is the chief officer, or attendant, of a mosque, and a cleric is a scholar of Islamic law. Together they make up the nearest arrangement in Islam that compares to an organized priesthood. Unlike priests, imams are not required to undergo any formal religious education or training. An imam is generally selected from the among the religious and respected men of the district surrounding the mosque.

The imam's main duty is to lead the prayers at a mosque, but he also has a role as an informal adviser on religious and personal matters. People will seek out the local imam if they have a matter they wish to discuss. On special occasions, the role of the imam at public prayers may be taken over by a distinguished visitor, someone noted for religious piety or scholarship.

Clerics, who are the learned interpreters of Islamic law, are known by more than one name. As a general group they are known as the *Ulema* ("OO-lay-mah"), while those who tend not to share their traditional attitudes sometimes refer to them as *mullahs* ("MOOL-lahs"). A cleric is revered not so much for his level of education as for his conservatism and his claim to know best how to interpret God's law. There is no simple distinction between law and religion in Pakistan, and consequently the clerics often perform a political role. In rural parts of the country their influence can be tremendous, and most local politicians would not wish to offend them unnecessarily.

RAMAZAN

Ramazan ("reh-meh-ZAHN") is the ninth month of the Moslem calendar and is the holy month of fasting. For 30 days, Moslems may not eat or drink from dawn to sunset. The only exceptions are nursing mothers and the sick, and they are expected to make up the lost days when able.

Ramazan changes every year, as the Islamic year is 11 days shorter than the Western year. Fasting is a very demanding requirement that calls for considerable self-discipline, yet the majority of Pakistanis endure it with goodwill. The country's productivity falls by 30% during Ramazan, and tempers fray toward evening, but it is very much a communal act of devotion. Each evening, once the *Azan* from the mosque has been announced, food stands everywhere are busy with customers, as the fast may now be broken. In the early hours of the morning, the women of the house are out of bed preparing a hot meal to be consumed before the sun rises.

The unrivalled Faisal Masjid in Islamabad occupies more than 626 thousand square feet. Its minarets are 290.4 feet high and have been compared to rockets because of their modernistic design. The mosque, which also houses an Islamic university, was named after King Faisal of Saudi Arabia. The Kingdom of Saudi Arabia provided most of the $50 million that went into the building of the mosque.

MOSQUES

The word "mosque" comes from the Arabic word *masjid* ("MEHZ-jid"), meaning "a place of kneeling," pointing to its primary function as a place for prayer. On Fridays, mosques throughout Pakistan are crowded with men coming to pray, but individuals stop in on other days of the week for private prayer or a quiet conversation with friends in the courtyard. Compared to European churches, interiors of mosques appear functional; a *mihrab* ("MIH-rahb"), which is a niche pointing toward Mecca in front of which the prayer leader stands, and a pulpit for the imam are the main features. The main aesthetic attraction is provided by the colorful artwork that decorate the walls. Outside the main entrance, and usually in a courtyard, a fountain is provided for the ceremonial washing before prayers.

A distinction can be made between the bigger types of mosques, known as Jamia mosques, and the numerous neighborhood ones that can be found close to a community or town. The Jamia Masjid in Karachi is one of the largest in the country, with a capacity of 10,000. Even this, however, is small compared to the Faisal Masjid in Islamabad. It is reputed to be the largest mosque in the world, holding over 15,000 people under a vast sweeping roof designed to resemble a desert tent.

Mosques have also developed social and educational functions. Groups of children are taken there after school for religious instruction, something like traditional Sunday school in the United States. In areas where there is no elementary school building, the mosque may serve that purpose. In the evening, groups of women may gather for their own religious instruction.

RELIGIOUS MINORITIES

Non-Moslems make up about 3% of the population. In Lahore and Karachi,
there are small communities of Parsis ("PAHR-sees") who practice one of
the oldest religions on earth, founded in the sixth or seventh century B.C.
Known also as Zoroastrianism, this religion once stretched from India to
the Mediterranean. Today it only survives in part of India, Iran, and
Pakistan. The Parsi god is symbolized by fire and flames burn continuously
in Parsi temples. Parsis believe that cremation or burial would result in the
pollution of the elements, and so they leave their dead in "Towers of
Silence," to be devoured by vultures and crows.

Christians form a large non-Moslem minority. Pakistani Christians tend
to be economically disadvantaged, the reason going back to British rule
when missionaries converted former Hindu untouchables to their faith. Of
the lowest Hindu caste, they were mostly poor and their descendants still
are today. They mostly worship in churches built by the British, although
a few new churches have been built.

LANGUAGE

OVER 300 DIALECTS AND LANGUAGES are spoken across Pakistan, and not one of them is spoken by the entire population. Not surprisingly, the variety of tongues is the main factor dividing the various cultural groups. As the groups are regional in nature, so too are their languages. Sindh is an exception to this. In recent years the region has received a substantial number of immigrants from other parts of the country. They come to Sindh because of the better employment opportunities in both the cities and the countryside and the native Sindhi language is spoken along with Punjabi and Urdu, making it easier for newcomers to adjust.

English was established as the language of bureaucracy and the law in the 1956 Constitution, and its official status was confirmed in the 1962 Constitution. The 1973 Constitution, however, set 1988 as the year in which Urdu would replace English as the official language. Since then the use of English has decreased considerably.

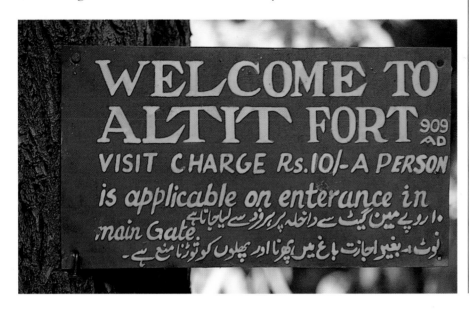

Opposite: **Girls doing their lessons in a rural school.**

Left: **A sign announcing admission charges for a tourist spot demonstrates the decline of English since Urdu was made the official language of Pakistan.**

URDU

Urdu is the country's official language, but it is not indigenous to Pakistan and is used as a first language by less than 10% of the population. This is despite the fact that it is the medium of instruction in schools. Urdu was the language of the educated Moslems of northern India, many of whom played large roles in the creation of Pakistan, and because of its nationalist connotations, it has been promoted as the unifying language.

Urdu is an old language with a literature of its own. Literary Urdu reveals Persian and Arabic influences, and this is the chief difference between Urdu and the Hindi language, which is written in a script descended from

Sanskrit. Urdu, which is descended from Hindi, took on many of its characteristic features soon after the arrival of Moslems in northern India in the 11th century. A large number of Arabic, Persian, and Turkish words entered Hindi through interaction with Moslem military camps and commercial dealings with traders. Over time, this hybrid language evolved into a separate dialect written in the Arabic script, with new letters added for sounds not represented in the original script. Eventually, this dialect became known as Urdu, meaning "camp language" in ancient Turkish, and spread to become the common language of Moslems over much of India.

In 1947, India adopted Hindi as its official language, and West Pakistan, now Pakistan, chose Urdu. Before Partition there was a term—Hindustani—which referred to both languages, but the need for this ended when India and Pakistan went their separate linguistic ways.

The Urdu script is written from right to left. The style is so elaborate that it is only quite recently that a typeface for it was devised. Before then the publication of anything in Urdu depended on the painstaking work of calligraphers.

PUNJABI

Punjabi, as the name implies, is spoken in the Punjab region, a historic territory that is now divided between Pakistan and India. Many different dialects of Punjabi are in use. A Pakistani speaker of Punjabi would not readily be able to understand all of what is said by an Indian speaker of the same tongue. One Punjabi dialect spoken in Pakistan, known as Lahnda, is considered sufficiently different from the mainstream language to warrant classification as a separate language.

Originally, the written Punjabi language was used to record the teachings of the 10 Sikh gurus, the founders of the Sikh religion. The alphabet, called Gurmukhi (which means "coming from the mouth of the guru"), was invented in the 16th century by one of these gurus. Gurmukhi is still used by Sikh Punjabi speakers in India. In Pakistan, there has been a movement to encourage the use of the Urdu script, in an attempt to disassociate from India and more closely identify Punjabi with Pakistan's official language.

SINDHI

This language is spoken by over eight million people in the southern Pakistani province of Sindh. Hyderabad, one of Pakistan's largest cities, has the greatest concentration of Sindhi speakers in the country. Across the border in India, there are an estimated two million speakers of the same language. Sindhi is related to Urdu, and in Pakistan it is written in a special variant of the Arabic script, with additional letters to accommodate special sounds. Two factors have contributed to the dilution of Sindhi, one being the number of non-Sindhi speakers who have settled in the province. Most urban areas now have a majority of Urdu speakers. The other factor goes back to the days of Partition in 1947, when many of the educated Sindhi speakers, who were Hindus, left the province for a new life in India.

Above: **Even though there are more than eight million Sindhi speakers in Pakistan, not many Sindhi books are published because of the emphasis on Urdu.**

Opposite: **Although the Punjabi language is still in use in Pakistan, children like this young Punjabi girl no longer learn to write in Gurmukhi, the original Punjabi script. The Urdu script is used instead.**

Gurmukhi	Sindhi
ਜੋ ਘਰਿ ਕੀਰਤਿ ਆਖੀਐ ਕਰਤੇ ਕਾ ਹੋਇ ਬੀਚਾਰੋ ॥ ਤਿਤੁ ਘਰਿ ਗਾਵਹੁ ਸੋਹਿਲਾ ਸਿਵਰਿਹੁ ਸਿਰਜਨਹਾਰੋ ॥੧॥ ਤੁਮ ਗਾਵਹੁ ਮੇਰੇ ਨਿਰਭਉ ਕਾ ਸੋਹਿਲਾ ॥ ਹਉਵਾਰੀ ਜਿਤੁ ਸੋਹਿਲੈ ਸਦਾ ਸੁਖੁ ਹੋਇ ॥੧॥ ਰਹਾਉ ॥ ਨਿਤ ਨਿਤ ਜੀਅੜੇ ਸਮਾ-ਲੀਅਨਿ ਦੇਖੈਗਾ ਦੇਵਣਹਾਰੁ ॥ ਤੇਰੇ ਦਾਨੈ ਕੀਮਤਿ ਨਾ ਪਵੈ ਤਿਸੁ	مونکي اڪرين . وڌا ٿورا لاٿا ۽ نه ڀٽ ٻس ، ڪٽان جي ڪر سامعون . اڪر يوں برين ري ، جي ڀي ٻيو ٻس ۽ نه ٻدي ڪي ڪاتگن ، ٻرا لا ٻٽ زبان . نن ٻيٽ حي ٻران ، جن ساجر سيٽ ساٻينا ۽ جي ، جسي پڃان ، ڇر حضري چ ڪبر . ٻ سن ٻهازي ، نو ۽ نرسن او نومن ۽ آيا سماني ، ٻيٽ ٻاري برين ڪي . اڪن ڪي آهين . عب جمڙ ٻون عادر نون ۽ سور براني سات جا وچيو وعماٿن . اني انزلا ٻين ، جن حاجت ناه هٻاري جي .

PUSHTO

Pushto is the language of the Pathans, and while it has been spoken by them for centuries, there is no written script of the language. Recently, in an attempt to remedy this and help preserve the rich oral tradition of the language, a modified Persian script has been introduced. The large numbers of Pushto-speaking Afghan refugees, who fled Afghanistan when the Soviet Union invaded it in late 1979, have helped spread the use of Pushto in Pakistan.

If you think you have had enough of the sweet tea or pastries that have been offered to you, just say "bus," *meaning "enough."*

ACH'HAA?

Despite the hundreds of languages and dialects spoken across Pakistan, there are certain words and phrases that are used and understood almost everywhere. *Roti* ("ROH-ti"), strictly speaking, means "bread," and it is understood as such almost everywhere. This flat bread, in all its versions, forms such a basic food in Pakistan that the word is sometimes used to represent the broader concept of "eating" or "a meal." So, for example, a traveler or guest may be invited to join a group of men eating by being greeted with the words *roti k'ha'o* ("ROW-ti KHAO"; literally "eat bread").

Even more ubiquitous is the use of the term *ach'ha* ("EHCH-ah") which, at its most basic, means "good." It has a far wider use, though, and includes the friendly and amicable spirit that Americans express when saying "OK" or "no problem." What really stretches its meaning, however, is the way one or both syllables can be drawn out to indicate varying shades of expression. A few examples follow:

Ach'haa?	Really?
Ach'hha	That's all.
Aach'ha!	Nothing more to say; that's OK; understood.
Ach'haha!	OK.
Ach'hhaah!	I'm shocked!

ARTS

IT IS THE EXTENSIVE ISLAMIC INFLUENCE that makes the arts of Pakistan so distinctive and interesting. Some of the art forms familiar to North Americans, like theater, are almost nonexistent and others, like popular music, are radically different. Islamic theologians have always prohibited artists from engaging in pictorial art because realistic paintings and statues might be seen as divine in their own right and divert attention from the worship of Allah. Also, Allah is regarded as the only creator of life, so any attempt to create realistic forms is seen as blasphemy. Although this has not always been followed, it does explain why the emphasis in Pakistani art is on non-pictorial forms.

DESIGN MOTIFS

Traditional Islamic art has been compared to modern forms of abstract art. Despite their divergent origins, the two approaches have in common an emphasis on abstract patterns and geometric shapes. The most distinctive Islamic art form is the arabesque, an ornamental style in which linear flowers, foliage, fruits, animals, and designs are represented in intricate patterns. The arabesque was introduced to the region around 1000 B.C. from the Middle East and is greatly in evidence in modern Pakistan.

The focus on geometric patterns and designs has produced what is probably the world's most complex and sophisticated development of this art form. People outside Pakistan are only able to appreciate it by way of lavishly illustrated books and visits to art museums. In Pakistan itself, the art is on public display in the colored tiles that decorate minarets of mosques and the incredibly elaborate designs that weave their way around the exterior and interior of mosques.

Opposite: **The ceiling of the Badshahi Masjid. Pakistani mosques are intricately decorated, making them works of art in themselves.**

Above: **A Pakistani putting the finishing touches on the tilework adorning the exterior of a mosque.**

CALLIGRAPHY

Islam endorses the use of the Arabic script, the language of the Koran, and this has allowed the art of beautiful writing to develop as an art form in itself. Short extracts from the Koran are written on large scrolls and hung in mosque interiors. The lavish flourishes of calligraphy are a beautiful sight even to the non-Moslem visitor. Sometimes the calligraphy is surrounded by elaborate designs or arabesques to complement the words.

There are two main styles of Arabic calligraphy: Kufi and Neskhi. The Kufi style is the older form. It developed in Iraq and spread eastward, and flourished until around the 12th century when the Neskhi style became more prevalent. Both scripts are used to make copies of the Koran, with the older style being reserved for the chapter headings. In Pakistan, calligraphy can also be found on non-religious objects like vases and plates.

POTTERY

Pottery is the oldest art in Pakistan, going back to the time of the Indus Valley civilization, as excavations at Mohenjo-Daro have revealed. Many of the techniques in use today were perfected more than 1,000 years ago in Syria and Iraq and brought to Pakistan by Moslem artists. Chief among these techniques are the engraving or painting of intricate lattice designs on the slip—the earthy coating of the object—and then the covering of the object with transparent glazes of different colors. Another technique, introduced into Pakistan from the Middle East and still practiced today, involves the application of

blue designs on white ceramic glazes—a demanding technique that Italian potters copied during the Renaissance.

The art of the potter is also in evidence in the beautiful tilework adorning the minarets and domes of mosques as well as the walls of public buildings. Tile-making is traditionally a family occupation, with the skills handed down from generation to generation. Around Hyderabad, such families still practice the techniques first acquired by their ancestors centuries ago.

An astonishing continuity in artistic traditions can be found in the work of contemporary potters applying their skills and imagination to the production of kitchen plates, vases, and other decorative items. Motifs and animal designs that were discovered in Mohenjo-Daro, and which date back nearly 5,000 years, including lattice designs, floral patterns, leopards, bulls, and rhinoceroses, still appear in the 1990s. The use of animal forms is an exception to the usual prohibition on realistic portrayals.

Traditionally, pottery skills were handed down from father to son, but today there are many women potters in Pakistan.

CARPET-MAKING

The close link between art and everyday life in Pakistan is dramatically apparent in the work of carpet-makers. Although carpet factories do exist, many people work in their own homes and take the finished product to a carpet company where it is checked for quality and then paid for. Whole families often work together to make carpets, and children are especially valued because their small hands and agile fingers are ideally suited to the tying of the fine knots used to create the patterns. Unfortunately, unscrupulous merchants employ children in factories for this type of work. The children are forced to work 12-hour days and are paid hardly anything. Sometimes parents sell off their own children for this kind of work in an attempt to pay outstanding debts.

Rugs and carpets are mostly made for daily use. In tribal areas they are woven from camel hair and wool and mixed with cotton. This type is known as the *farashi* ("ferh-AHSH-ee") rug. The patterns are never written down. The women who do the weaving discuss the choice of colors and patterns among themselves before starting work.

The designs and patterns that carpet-makers employ vary from region to region. In regions that border on Afghanistan, the Kalashnikov rifle has appeared as a symbol on carpets, reflecting the war that followed the Soviet Union's invasion of that country. Certain basic designs and motifs are ubiquitous—wavy lines with abstract patterns, geometric shapes enclosed in squares, scrolls with rolled up ends, octagons—but the scope for variation and invention seems endless and identical carpets, other than from the same factory or family, never seem to appear.

Very expensive carpets may take as long as a year to complete. Such a carpet will sell for $25,000 in Pakistan and perhaps twice that much by the time it reaches an exclusive showroom in New York or London.

ARCHITECTURE

Classic Pakistani architecture manifests itself in the design of mosques and ancient buildings from the Moghul past.

The Shah Jehan Masjid in Sindh is the most glorious example of Pakistan's ecclesiastical architecture. The popular story behind its construction is that Shah Jehan was so grateful for the help he was given by the local people during the war of succession after his father's death that he designed and built this mosque as an expression of his gratitude.

The building is impressively large, approximately 19,800 square feet in area, with over 90 domed compartments that help spread sound throughout the mosque. The acoustics are such that prayers recited in front of the mihrab travel around the whole building and can be heard in every corner. The entire interior is decorated with superb, painstaking craftwork—in the artwork of the pillars, the intricate patterns in the tiles, the glazed bricks of various hues that catch the light, and the beautiful calligraphy that adorns the gold-colored stonework everywhere. The carving of the stone is so fine and delicate in places that from a short distance it would seem to be the work of a sculptor working with soft wood.

The ancient city of Lahore is particularly rich with examples of the country's architectural past. The greatest of the Moghul emperors, Akbar, made it his capital from 1584 to 1598 and started building the Lahore Fort. It was added to during the reigns of Jahangir and Shah Jehan.

The Lahore Fort remains an eloquent testimonial to these illustrious rulers and also to a group of anonymous 16th-century architects. The fort covers an area of 30 acres and the buildings inside its walls serve to remind one of the rigorous class system that prevailed at the time. A special raised balcony was built in the *Diwan-e-Aam* ("di-WAHN-e-ahm"), the Hall of Public Audience, so that the powerful emperor could look down over his subjects who came to present petitions and beg for a favorable judgment in their disputes. For wealthier subjects who were landlords and rulers in their own right, the *Diwan-e-Khas* ("di-WAHN-e-khahs"), the Hall of Special Audience, was built—a floor above the Diwan-e-Aam.

Compared with the strict functionality of these features, the Shish Mahal—the Palace of Mirrors—is an extravagant outburst of the imagination. It was built as a home for the empress and consists of a row of domed rooms with high roofs covered with hundreds of thousands of tiny mirrors. The mirror mosaics are in the style of the traditional Punjabi craft of *Shishgari* ("shish-GARI"), the designing of patterns from fragments of mirrors.

If not for the Taj Mahal in India, which Shah Jehan also designed, the Shah Jehan Masjid would be looked upon as his greatest architectural achievement. His reign, from 1627 to 1658, is synonymous with the finest expression of Moghul art.

METALWORK AND JEWELRY

Metalwork, like other arts and crafts in Pakistan, bridges the division between objects for everyday use and *objets d'art*. Platters and trays designed to be used in the home are often beautifully engraved with floral designs and intricate scrolls tapped out with light blows from a small hammer. Every large town has a shopping area where metalworkers sit cross-legged on cushions while they hammer out their craft on finely worked plates, teapots, vases, and other household utensils.

There is also a flourishing custom for decorative metalworked items, many of which are copies of famous medieval pieces of art. Different regions are famous for their expertise in highly specialized branches of metalwork. Certain towns in Punjab, for instance, are renowned for their damascene work on metal ornaments inlaid with gold or silver. Another speciality is silver inlay on a metal amalgam, producing a startling contrast between the silver and the dark metal. Expert filigree work, using fine wire strands of gold, silver, or copper to form delicate tracery, appears on window frames, grills, and folding screens.

Jewelry is held in high regard and pieces are treasured and kept for generations. They are worn with pride by women, and often represent the entire wealth of a family. Poor families would never think of parting with valuable items of family jewelry. Chokers, earrings, bracelets, and necklaces are often made of solid silver, inlaid with emeralds and rubies.

A man works painstakingly to engrave a tray with a verse from the Koran.

POPULAR ART

Popular art is on display, not in art galleries, but on the sides, backs, and fronts of the myriad vehicles found on the streets of Pakistan. The fascination with abstract forms and creative play of colors and shapes is readily apparent here as well. The major difference is that more realistic portraits of people and places appear, as though the strictures of Islam that normally discourage such pictures did not apply in this context.

The paintings that sometimes adorn every available inch of space on a truck or bus are only realistic in the sense that the subject matter can be easily recognized, like a mountain landscape or a lush valley. Just as

Trucks and buses have become, literally, the art galleries of Pakistan.

identifiable are the animals and fish that crowd in on one another like a crazily packed zoo. But this is where the photographic realism ends, for the colors and motifs that are also present go well beyond what is pictorially correct. Sunsets are not just red but flaming red, as if the earth were on fire. The colors used to paint animals are exotic, and the mixing of animals with floral patterns and stylized hearts, all enclosed within a waving border of lurid shapes, is surreal.

Religious symbolism is not absent. The word "Allah" in the Arabic script is a recurring presence, surrounded by floral displays or framed by an arabesque. Often verses from the Koran are painted on. A popular one is the prayer asking Allah to keep travelers safe.

QAWWALIS

Qawwalis ("keh-WAH-lees") are the mystic songs of Sufi poets, characterized by the rhythmic chanting of repeated phrases to the accompaniment of music. The singers of these devotional songs are called *qawwals*, and their aim is to strengthen the conviction of believers and convert nonbelievers to Islam. Traditionally, musical accompaniment is played on a *sarangi* ("SAH-rehng-gi"), but as this sometimes takes a half hour to retune between songs, modern performers prefer to use the harmonium instead. The harmonium is a cross between the organ and the piano accordion and is said to have been introduced to South Asia by Portuguese Jesuit missionaries who were seeking to spread Christianity.

A contemporary *qawwali* band consists of a lead singer, known as the *mohri* ("MO-ri"), two harmonium players, a backup singer, and a hand-clapping chorus. *Qawwals* sing both ancient and modern *qawwalis*, and a contemporary *qawwali* band like Nusrat Ali Khan's will compose new songs and the music to accompany them. Sometimes, as in jazz, new compositions emerge during a performance. *Qawwalis* are sung in Persian, Punjabi, or Urdu, and are usually staged on a Thursday evening, the eve of Islam's holy day, at a shrine or a Sufi meeting place. Women cannot become *qawwals*, although they can sing in movies as well as perform folk and classical songs.

The lyrics are usually devotional in nature, praising Allah, Mohammed, or Ali. Others praise the saints who introduced Sufism into the region. The poetry behind the devotion can be appreciated even in translation, with lines like "The dust of his footsteps is fragrant to my ears" and "Since you, my beloved, fell out with me, the crows no longer come to croak on the little wall."

KING OF QAWWALIS

Nusrat Ali Khan is Pakistan's premier *qawwal*. Born in 1948, he is the son of a famous classical musician who was also a *qawwal*. His father, realizing how demanding his own work was, wanted his son to study medicine. But the young Nusrat was captivated by the sound of his father's singing and started to take lessons. Today Nusrat is known as "*Shahen-Shah*"—meaning "The King of Kings"—and has received numerous awards, both in his own country and abroad. He was given the title "The Pride of Performance" by the country and more recently he has been dubbed "King of Qawwalis."

Nusrat Ali Khan performs in Pakistan and abroad, attracting a full house wherever he is and frequently attracting non-Moslems to his international concerts. He says, "It's great that even people who don't understand the language appreciate the music. It doesn't need words. I convey the message of the Sufi, the saints, but my music is not just for Moslems, but for anyone who believes in God. It's open to anyone."

Nusrat's band is made up of family members, and in Pakistan, they release a new audio tape every three months. For the international market, they have brought out record collections titled *Shahen-Shah* and *Mustt Mustt*.

LEISURE

MOST FAMILIES cannot afford to spend much money on leisure activities, and children are generally left on their own to develop enjoyable pastimes.

Kite flying is popular throughout the country. Kites are often homemade, and children learn through experience how to apply the aeronautical principles that make a successful kite. A discarded plastic bag and carefully selected twigs will be fashioned into a kite with the judicious use of glue, and it is a matter of pride to make one that stays aloft for more than just a short while.

Other games popular with young people include marbles and something that resembles hopscotch. In the cities there are more opportunities for entertainment, usually on Thursday afternoon and all day Friday. This is the Pakistani weekend, and a coastal city like Karachi will have camel and horse rides on the beach, family picnics in the public gardens, and an amusement park with bumper cars and train rides.

Opposite: **Field hockey is a popular sport in Pakistan, especially with schoolchildren, and this has spawned a huge demand for hockey sticks.**

Left: **A young boy realizes what fun it is to splash around in the canals that are part of the irrigation system in Punjab.**

While every school will have fields for cricket, field hockey and soccer, the necessary facilities for tennis and squash are usually only available in private clubs. The club membership fees mean, in effect, that only a tiny minority of Pakistanis have the opportunity to play.

SPORTS

Cricket is the national sport, but other games are also played. Field hockey and soccer feature on the timetable of most schools, and although Pakistan's national soccer team has not achieved any notable success, the country's field hockey team is always a force to be reckoned with in international competitions. Volleyball, tennis, and squash are also popular games, and Pakistan is frequently the world champion in squash.

There are very few organized sports for women, apart from badminton and table tennis, which are played in schools and colleges. Moslem clerics tend to frown on the idea of women participating in any public sport.

Outside the towns and cities, and apart from school events, there is little organized sport. One of the most popular village sports is cockfighting. Roosters have special small spurs fitted to their legs and before they battle it out, sometimes fatally, the spectators place their illicit bets. A less bloody sport is *kabaddi* ("ka-BAD-i"), a form of wrestling that is especially popular in the Punjab.

POLO Polo is a stick-and-ball game played on horseback by teams of four players—although Pakistani teams tend to have at least six. The playing area, the largest for any ball game, is 300 yards by 160 yards, although often the boundaries are not fixed and play extends over an even wider area. The object of the game is to strike the ball with a hand-held mallet into the opposing eight-yard-wide and 10-foot-high goal. Each game is divided into seven-minute periods known as *chukkas* ("CHUCK-ahs"), and the number of *chukkas* in a game varies from one competition to another.

Polo was first played in Central Asia around 500 B.C. When the game traveled east to the land south of the Himalayas, it took a firm hold and when the British colonized the Indian subcontinent, they discovered the game and took to it with enthusiasm. It became a popular game with the British army, and most of the best polo teams today come from the armed forces of the United Kingdom. This is only partly due to an inherited tradition, for while only wealthy individuals can afford the luxury of owning their own horses, the army and the police play as team members on horses that are not personally owned.

Polo is most popular in the northern areas of Pakistan, and large crowds will turn up for the breathtaking displays of horsemanship that are a guaranteed feature of every game. The boundary is usually a low-lying wall and the audience crowds dangerously close to this wall to follow the progress of the game as the ball is hurtled around the field and bounced off the wall at high speed.

Between 1960 and 1978, no cricket was played between Pakistan and India due to the dispute over Kashmir.

CRICKET Cricket was developed in England in the mid-16th century. It is a bat-and-ball game similar to baseball, with each team of 11 players taking turns to bat and bowl. The batting team's objective is to defend the wicket, made up of three wooden stumps placed at either end of a grassy 22-yard pitch, against the bowler of the opposing team, who throws a small heavy ball at the wicket. If the batsman hits the ball away, he can then run to the other end of the pitch and score a "run." The British introduced the game to the region, and Pakistan now has one of the best cricket teams in the world.

It would be difficult to be in Pakistan between October and March without realizing that cricket season was in progress. If Pakistan is playing at home in a test match, the host city often declares the final day of the match a school holiday. While the game itself may be played in Lahore, almost 500 miles away, near the Afghan border, tribe members will huddle around a radio listening with bated breath and roaring with delight at every run scored by their country's team.

While the commentary to an international match is blaring from every radio and television set in the country, boys will be lined up in teams, playing the game in a nearby field or side street. They hope to emulate their country's great cricket stars, who, unlike the majority of Pakistanis who achieve fame and fortune, were not born in the lap of luxury and privilege.

Sometimes, the excitement and passion generated by a game of cricket goes beyond the matter of sport. Any encounter between the national teams of Pakistan and India can take on political overtones, especially if the political relationship between the two countries happens to be particularly heightened at the time. In 1986, when Pakistan for the first time defeated India in a series played on Indian territory, the returning heroes were greeted by a crowd of over a quarter of a million.

CRICKET SUPERSTARS

Hanif Mohammad (1934–)

Hanif Mohammad holds two world records in cricket. Playing in a match between Karachi and Bahawalpur, he was running for his 500th run when the ball hit the wicket before he could reach it. The 499 runs represents the highest score ever reached in first-class cricket. In 1958, playing for his country against the West Indies, he conducted the longest innings—scoring 337 runs over a period of 16 hours and 10 minutes.

Hanif Mohammad's three brothers also played cricket for Pakistan. By the time he retired in 1969, he had obtained centuries (100 runs a game) playing against all the major cricket nations except South Africa, which Pakistan had refused to play against. Hanif Mohammad was small for a cricketer and this earned him the nickname "Little Master."

Imran Khan (1952–)

Imran Khan is considered to be one of the world's greatest all-rounders in the history of modern cricket. His fast bowling is feared by opposing batsmen, while he himself is well-known for his attacking style when batting. In addition, he is a highly prized fielder.

Imran Khan was 18 when he first played for his country against England, and by the time he retired from the game he had won numerous awards and distinctions. At the end of 1987, when the captain of the national cricket team resigned, there were demonstrations outside Imran Khan's house calling for him to return to the game and captain the Pakistani team against the West Indies. Some fans even threatened to go on hunger strikes until he agreed to return! Eventually, after President Zia also called for his return, Khan agreed to come out of retirement.

According to the Guinness Book of Records, the greatest victory in cricket was when Pakistani Railways beat Dera Ismail Khan (another Pakistani team) by 851 runs at Lahore in 1964.

MOVIES AND TELEVISION

If a family possesses a television set and a program is being broadcast, then the television will almost certainly be on. And it will stay on until the last broadcast is over. People do not necessarily watch what is on, and may go about their business—talking, sewing, cooking, and so on—only occasionally pausing to watch something of interest. If visitors come into the house, the television will not be turned off or down, but simply ignored.

In the countryside, television viewing has become the main leisure activity in the evening. In the past, farmers would go to bed soon after nightfall because there was little else to do, but now the television monopolizes their time until around 11 p.m. when transmission usually ends. Friends and neighbors who do not possess their own sets will drop in to watch their favorite programs.

Boys on bicycles selling pictures of movie stars are a common sight in cities.

A lot of television time is taken up with religious programs consisting of long sermons or readings from the Koran. While readings from the Koran are treated with grave respect, the sermons by *mullahs* are sometimes so lengthy the people joke that they can see the *mullah's* beard growing during the course of his talk. More popular are the game shows, soap operas, and dramas that are churned out with relentless regularity

from the movie and television studios in Lahore and elsewhere.

Movies are not made one at a time, as in the West, and a big star is often involved in a number of movies at the same time. The typical movie is a rich mixture of action, drama, suspense, romance, music, and dancing. It is a genre in its own right, with conventions that every Pakistani will understand and appreciate. An action sequence involving a high-speed car chase may be quickly followed by a scene in a rural setting with the hero being sung to by a group of dancing females. This may then be followed by the star singing a solo number in a very romantic mood, only to be followed by gunfire and a fistfight.

In the cities, going to the movies is a favorite form of entertainment. A new movie featuring one of the country's movie stars will attract huge crowds, and posters of the star will be on sale everywhere.

Crowds of people flock to movie theaters on the weekend. Movie-going is a favorite pastime for both old and young.

103

STORYTELLING

Each cultural group has its own folk literature that has been passed down from one generation to the next by word of mouth. Stories about legendary or historical figures are still told by semi-professional storytellers whose skill is not in telling a new story, but in retelling a familiar tale in a new style. Changes in the tone of voice, body language, and anecdotal extras all contribute to the audience's entertainment. Unfortunately, this tradition is now being eroded by the spread of television.

Punjab is especially rich in its store of romantic tales, and a recurring theme is that of doomed lovers thwarted by fate and parents who cannot understand the force of their children's feelings. The most enduring romance of them all is the story of Heer and Ranjha.

Men gather after work to listen to a storyteller.

HEER AND RANJHA

It was love at first sight when Ranjha first gazed into the eyes of the beautiful Heer. Ranjha was wandering aimlessly, having left his home after a family dispute. One day he came to a river and boarded a ferry, tired and exhausted after days of walking through unknown territory.

There was a bed on the boat belonging to Heer, and the boatman reluctantly agreed to let his passenger sleep there. When Hir boarded the boat, she was shocked to find a strange man in her bed. Her scolding awakened Ranjha, who opened his eyes to the sight of Heer and could only exclaim, "Oh, beloved!" She too fell in love instantly.

Each afternoon the lovers would meet by the river. Their love was kept a secret until a vindictive uncle told Heer's father what was happening. Ranjha was immediately expelled from the village and the heartbroken Heer was forced to marry a man she did not love.

Ranjha sought help from holy men and a plan was worked out that involved Heer's sister-in-law, who also planned to run away with her lover. The four young people all ran away the same night, but Heer and Ranjha were caught and put on trial. When it was revealed that Heer had been forced into marriage, her marriage was declared invalid and Ranjha and Heer were free to marry.

However, the wicked uncle convinced Heer's father that her honor had been violated. As Hir prepared for her wedding day, she was offered a poisoned drink and fell dead. Ranjha rushed to her tomb and, torn by grief and feeling there was no reason left to live, he fell dead upon her grave.

FESTIVALS

THE MAJOR FESTIVALS in Pakistan are all religious, although there are many rural festivals that are more secular in nature. In the north of the country, the coming of spring will often be celebrated by locally organized competitions. Pairs of oxen are yoked to the wheel of the village well and timed to see how long they take to complete a set number of turns. Music and fireworks add to the festivities. The day is welcomed by farming people who work hard throughout the year and have little leisure time. Later in the year, at harvest time, local festivals will be held again to mark the successful conclusion of another summer's work. In Punjab, this is the time when singers and storytellers bring traditional myths and legends to life. A popular folk dance is the Bhangra, and it is usually featured at Punjabi harvest festivals. It is a dance performed in a circle, and both men and women take part. Even if the harvest has been a poor one and the crop yield a disappointment, there will still be a festival. Pakistanis have a strong belief in fate and do not look to blame someone for an event seen as part of God's plan.

Many festivals vary from one region to another. In a northern area called Hunza, the autumn festival celebrates the return of the herdsmen from the higher pastures, and a sword dance is performed. The sword dance harks back to the lawless days of this once inaccessible region, when a man's survival depended on his ability to handle a sword in close combat.

The two major religious festivals are the two Eids. The "Small Eid" celebrates the end of Ramadan, the fasting month, and 10 weeks later the "Big Eid" commemorates Abraham's willingness to slaughter his own son in obedience to God.

Opposite: **A young girl is dressed up in her new clothes in celebration of Eid ul-Fiter, the end of the fasting month.**

Above: **During their spring festival, the Kalash women take to the dancing ground and perform traditional dances that have always excluded men.**

At Lahore's Badshahi Masjid on the eve of Eid, the courtyard of more than six acres fill up long before sunrise and so do the surrounding gardens and streets. A crowd of 300,000 is not unusual.

EID UL-FITER

Young people always look forward to the Small Eid, the *Eid ul-Fiter* ("eed ool-FIT-erh"), because it is the time of the year when they receive a new set of clothes and gifts of money. It is more like Christmas in the West than any other Pakistani festival. Employees receive bonuses, factories and offices close down for a couple of days, and food and money are distributed to the poor.

Eid ul-Fiter, celebrated throughout the Moslem world, is the most festive day on the Islamic calendar. On the eve of Eid, thousands of Pakistanis set out on lengthy journeys to pray at one of the bigger mosques.

Because it marks the end of Ramadan, the Small Eid is always an occasion for a celebratory meal, and families come together in the spirit of the American Thanksgiving.

On the first day of the festival, all the male members of a household visit a mosque for special morning prayers. Immediately after, they visit friends and relatives. Children, dressed in their best new clothes and looking forward to receiving gifts of money, also go visiting. During the festival the Pakistani love of costume is displayed to its best advantage by the various ethnic groups. Punjabi males wear new turbans, Pathan tribesmen carry their best rifles, the barrels often painted, and even camels will be adorned with gaudy trappings. The women wear their best *shalwar kamiz*. Those who wear head-to-toe *burquahs* dress in colorful new robes, while other women don new gowns of fine embroidered silk.

EID UL-AZHA

Eid ul-Azha ("eed ool-a-ZAH"), also known as the Big Eid, is the celebration of Abraham's willingness to sacrifice his son Isaac in obedience to Allah. It is marked by the slaughtering of a male goat, sheep, or calf. Despite the cost, this is something no family will forego willingly.

The day itself begins like the Small Eid, with the men and boys going to the mosque for special prayers. When returning home they will bring with them a butcher to kill the animal if they are not doing it themselves. Whoever carries out the killing will preface the act with the word *"Bismillah"* ("bis-mill-LAH")—"in the name of Allah."

The sacrificial meat is cut into three main portions: for the family, for the relatives, and for the underprivileged. Charitable institutions receive large amounts of meat on this occasion. On the days that follow the average family consumes more meat than at any other time of the year.

During both Eids, the usual greeting is *"Eid mubarak"* ("eed moo-BAH-rak"), meaning "an auspicious Eid to you."

Fat decorated goats are on sale everywhere in the days immediately preceding Eid ul-Azha.

MUHARRAM

On Ashura, devout Shiites participate in processions to commemorate Imam Hussein's martyrdom. Some extreme devotees participate in self-flagellation in identification with Hussein's suffering.

On the 10th day of Muharram, the first month of the Moslem calendar, the death of Imam Hussein is marked. Hussein was killed 1,300 years ago in the cause of Islam, during the religious dissension that inaugurated the split between the Sunnis and the Shiites. Within the Shiites there is another division, between "Twelver" Shiites and the Ismailis. The "Twelver" group believes that the line of living imams came to an end with the 12th, while the Ismailis believe that the line continued.

The mourning begins on the first day of the month for Shiite Moslems, but the culmination of the festival is on the 10th day, known as *Ashura* ("AH-shoo-rah"). On this day there are large public processions held in all parts of the country where "Twelver" Shiites are found. The most dramatic feature of the day is the self-flagellation that some devotees suffer as an act of pious identification with the sufferings of Hussein. Each procession has a section where believers volunteer to have their backs beaten with special whips and chains that contain five short, sharp blades at the end. Some members of the procession collapse from shock after the loss of blood, but they are quickly replaced by others, all crying "Ya Hussein."

Sunnis commemorate the death of Hussein in a less dramatic manner. For the first 10 days of the month all forms of public entertainment, including the playing of music, are shut down.

NATIONAL HOLIDAYS

March 23	Pakistan Day: The commemoration of the Pakistan Resolution passed in 1940 calling for a separate Moslem state.
May 1	Labor Day.
August 14	Independence Day: The commemoration of the founding of Pakistan in 1947.
September 6	Defense of Pakistan Day: The commemoration of the 1965 Indo-Pakistani War.
September 11	The anniversary of the death of Muhammad Ali Jinnah.
November 9	Iqbal Day: The birthday of celebrated Urdu poet Allama Iqbal.
December 25	The birthday of Muhammad Ali Jinnah.

MELAS

Melas ("MEL-ahs") is the general word for the fairs that take place throughout the country at different times of the year. They are not national events and generally attract only the local population. To the visitor they often seem to represent a mix of the religious and the secular. Traders set up more stalls in the market than usual, and a traveling circus may erect its tents to display dancing bears and monkeys. A merry-go-round is nearly always put up in the town or village square, to be followed by swings and slides. Women and children arrive at these *melas* in large groups.

In many areas, the *melas* are the largest shopping days of the year, and many traders, like this carpet seller, set up stands to display their wares.

There may also be an air of religious frenzy as people engage in chanting and ritual dancing. The biggest and most dramatic *melas* are those associated with Sufi saints. Every village in Pakistan has its own small shrine dedicated to a local saint, and every saint has his *urs*, the annual celebration dedicated to the memory of the holy man. Some of these festivals attract thousands of devotees from all over the country.

During an *urs*, a wedding procession takes place, representing the saint's communion with Allah.

URS

The mausoleum of Sheikh Osman, known as Shah Lal Baz Qalandar, located in Sindh, is the site of an annual three-day festival. What is unusual about Osman is that he is revered by both Moslems and Hindus. There are three guardians of Osman's shrine—one Moslem and two Hindus. The position of guardian of the shrine is a hereditary one and remains in the same family for as long as there is a male to inherit the role.

Osman's death is commemorated by the enactment of a marriage ceremony representing the saint's communion with God. On the first day, a marriage procession travels from the home of the Moslem guardian to the flower-laden tomb. Marriage processions are also carried out on the second and third days, starting from the homes of the Hindu guardians. Hindu and Moslem pilgrims come from all parts of Sindh and beyond, and for three days the air is full of music, dancing, and singing. In the courtyard of the mausoleum, large copper drums are beaten constantly as devotees make their way to the shrine. Both men and women dance, a traditional ritual set of movements that propel the dancer forward and backward with hands held high in the air. Osman is also the special saint to groups of singing women who have their own ritual display of song and dance that seeks to emulate the religious ecstasy of the moment of union with God.

BASANT FESTIVAL

This colorful festival takes place at the beginning of March in the city of Lahore and marks the coming of spring. It is not a religious event and is celebrated by a great display of kite flying. Big fields, as well as rooftops, become the locations for large-scale kite flying competitions. There are different competitions for different categories of kites, from small ones to those over three feet long. Some of the kites are square, others the double-bodied type known as *toukal* ("TOO-kahl"), and every color of the rainbow is seen fluttering in the sky.

What adds excitement to the competitions is the fact that the kite strings are coated with ground glass, and the object is to try and ground competitors' kites by cutting their strings in the air. Serious kite flyers wear gloves to protect their hands. Every time a kite string is cut, a tremendous roar goes up from the appreciative crowd. Drums and trumpets are played to make sure everyone knows another competitor has been knocked out of the game. As the player's friends offer their sympathy, children run through the streets trying to capture the kite if it falls to the ground. Some owners, having carefully constructed their kites, do not want to lose them and join the children in looking for their kites.

The festival lasts all day, and in the evening food stands are crowded with competitors and spectators. The following morning children can be seen climbing up the telephone poles and trees, trying to collect the fallen kites.

Kite flying is taken very seriously, with competitors' kite strings coated with ground glass in order to cut the string of other competitors' kites and knock them out of the competition.

113

FOOD

THE FOOD OF PAKISTAN shares a common heritage with India, but there are a number of factors that distinguish the two cuisines and which help to identify the special nature of Pakistani food. One of the factors stems from the Islamic ban on the eating of pork, and as the country is a Moslem state, this means that hardly any pork is ever eaten in Pakistan.

While India also has a large Moslem population, it is still only one component in the country's dietary makeup. Indian food also has a strong vegetarian influence, whereas their northern neighbors love meat. The typical Pakistani is not a vegetarian.

A distinguishing influence on Pakistani food are the Middle Eastern cuisines of Persia (modern Iran), Turkey, and the Arab states. The generous use of yogurt comes from these countries to the west of Pakistan and tends to have a cooling effect on the heat generated by the equally generous use of chili peppers.

Opposite: **A store selling the chili peppers and other spices which are basic ingredients in Pakistani cuisine.**

MOGHUL CUISINE

The term "Moghul food," with its aristocratic and exotic connotations, has become a general term for the style of cooking commonly found in Pakistan and northern India. To the average Westerner the food both sounds and tastes incredibly rich. Saffron, cardamom, turmeric, and ginger are relatively expensive herbs and spices in the West and used sparingly, whereas in Pakistan many of these are standard ingredients. Some of the more expensive items, like saffron, are not readily available to ordinary people in Pakistan either, but the typically rich and hot curry taste can be produced by easily available chili peppers, garlic, onions, and tomatoes.

The basic curry consists of onions and tomatoes cooked with small amounts of meat with spices and herbs in oil. What often lends a distinguished look to a curry is the garnish. Curries are garnished with a rich and varied selection of fruits, vegetables, and other food items. Raisins, cashew nuts, pistachios, eggs, and lettuce usually accompany curries served at special meals or feasts.

Bread is an important part of the Pakistani diet.

BREAD AND RICE

About 98% of the daily diet of most Pakistanis consists of four basic items: roti (bread), rice, vegetables, and some meat.

Roti comes in a variety of forms, of which *naan* ("NAHN") is the most common. Countless versions of the naan, a leavened flat bread, exist across a wide region stretching from the southern regions of the former Soviet Union to north India. In Pakistan it is eaten for breakfast, lunch, or dinner, and can accompany nearly every dish. It is baked in a special oven, the tandoor, which is about 48 inches deep and 39 inches wide. A small coal or gas fire burns under the oven. The professional naan-maker, the tandoori, shapes his bread to a thickness of about half an inch before placing it on a pan. He then hurls the bread against the hot sides of the oven, removing it later by means of a pair of iron tongs.

Paratha ("peh-RAH-thah"), a wholewheat griddle bread, is a close competitor of naan for popularity in Pakistan. Along with regular wholewheat flour, *chapati* ("cheh-PAH-ti") flour, which is made from a

THE NATIONAL DRINK

Most Pakistanis, being Moslems, do not drink alcohol. Tea, known as *chai* ("CHAI"), is the most common beverage. It is drunk at home, in restaurants, in the street from chai stalls, and even in shops where the proprietor is happy to make his potential customers relax by offering them a drink. It generally comes with the milk already added and is usually heavily sweetened. Spices like nutmeg, cinnamon, or cloves are sometimes added. After a meal, jasmine tea is sometimes served.

wheat very low in gluten, can be used. The basic paratha mix can be turned into a light puff pastry or a heavier, thicker version—both kinds can be served stuffed with minced meat and vegetables. Every home will have in its kitchen a rimless iron pan that is used for cooking the paratha or the thinner chapati. The skilful part of cooking these breads is in the kneading of the dough; the correct consistency must be reached before beating the dough into flat discs ready for cooking on both sides.

Special breads include *shirmal* ("SHERH-mahl"), cooked with milk and eggs, and *roghni* ("ROGUE-nee"), a soft and sweetish bread that accompanies many meat dishes.

Rice is the other staple in the Pakistani diet, and like bread, it comes in a variety of forms. Apart from plain white rice, one of the internationally known varieties is *biryani* ("bir-YAH-nee") rice. This is cooked in a meat sauce and is a favorite dish across the country for special events and festive meals. At its most attractive it is served with decorative pieces of edible silver paper that have a yellowish tinge due to the addition of a tiny amount of saffron. Even a plain-looking dish of white rice can taste delightful because of the judicious addition of cloves, cardamom, and cinnamon.

This fruit seller sits amid his wares, patiently awaiting a customer.

SHOPPING FOR FOOD

People in Pakistan buy their food in the local bazaar, a huddle of food stands and other small shops. Shops of the same kind are usually grouped together, so the meat-sellers will be in one group, fish vendors will occupy another area, and various displays of herbs and spices will also be found alongside each other.

An interesting feature of many meat and fish stands is the way the meat is cut up. The vendor squats on a small platform behind his cutting table, and customers find themselves at eye level with him. The meat or fish is purchased by weight and usually needs to be cut up in small pieces ready for cooking. A large razor-sharp knife is held between the large and index toe of one foot. The vendor simply holds the meat in front of the knife and moves it around, its size determining how many cuts are required. More modern stands have a large, curved knife fixed in position on the table.

In every bazaar there are stands that sell only roti and curry, the Pakistani equivalent of fast food. Practiced hands slap the bread dough around with the speed and expertise that only come from experience. As the chapati or paratha sizzles away, or the naan is reaching perfection, the vendor will spoon an amount of lentil or bean curry into thin plastic bags where it will keep warm.

Fast food is also readily available on the streets of most towns from vendors who peddle their food from mobile carts. They are often found around schools at the end of the day, ready for the onslaught of schoolchildren hungry after a hard day of studying.

GLOSSARY OF INGREDIENTS

Saffron: This is obtained from the orange-red stigmas of an Asian crocus. It is very expensive, as 150,000 flowers are required to produce two pounds of saffron. Fortunately, only a pinch adds an intriguing taste to whatever is being cooked; when added to rice it produces a golden color.

Cardamom: This is a tropical, perennial shrub, a member of the ginger family. Its aromatic seeds are highly flavored. It is a basic ingredient of any Pakistani curry and is generally sold in its pod.

Turmeric: This is a rhizome of the ginger family. When fresh, it resembles fine, ginger-like fingers and is bright yellow on the inside. It is also available ground, as a yellow powder.

Coriander: This herb is used all across Asia, and while most countries just use the leaves, in Pakistan the stalks are also used to add flavor to curry stock. It is also known as cilantro or Chinese parsley.

Amchoor: This is made from sour, unripe mangoes and adds a slightly sweet-sour taste.

KEEMA MATTER PILAU

3 cups long-grain rice
3 tablespoons oil or ghee
1 teaspoon cumin seeds
1 medium onion, finely chopped
1 clove garlic, crushed
$1/2$ teaspoon fresh ginger, finely grated
6 whole cloves
8 ounces ground beef
2 cups shelled green peas
4 cups hot water
3 tablespoons salt
1 teaspoon *garam masala* (powdered spice mix available at oriental groceries)

Wash rice if necessary and leave to drain. Heat ghee or oil in a large, heavy saucepan with a tightly fitting lid. Fry cumin seeds, onion, garlic, ginger, and cloves until onion is soft and golden brown. Add meat and fry over moderately high heat until meat is browned. Add peas and half a cup of water, stir well, cover and cook until peas are half done. Add rice and hot water and stir in salt. Bring quickly to a boil, cover, turn heat very low and cook for about 10 minutes. Uncover and sprinkle with *garam masala*. Do not stir. Replace lid and continue cooking for another 10 minutes or until the liquid is all absorbed and the rice is cooked through. Serves four.

PAKISTANI DISHES

BREAKFAST

Nihari: This is a meat mixture made of beef, brain, tongue, and marrow blended together in gravy. It is often eaten with naan.

Halwa-puri: This is a lighter breakfast dish. Small balls of wheat dough are slapped and smacked into paper-thin discs that are fried in oil, where they puff out like small footballs. They are made at home, but many people buy them from a food stand where they are served with lentils and gravy.

LUNCH OR DINNER

Korma: Spiced meat served with yogurt sauce in a thick gravy; a favorite meal.

Machli ka salan: A fish curry.

Haleem: A luxurious dish made of meat that has been cooked in seven grains including rice, different types of lentils, and wheat.

Tikka kebabs: Cubes of meat barbecued on skewers or baked in the tandoor oven.

Raita: This yogurt sauce, seasoned with delicate combinations of chili peppers, coriander, and pepper, is the most common accompaniment to a hot curry and rice. Subtle variations in the taste are obtained by imaginative additions to the basic ingredients.

DESSERT

Mithai: This is made from lentil flour, cooked in syrup, and comes in a variety of bright colors.

Barfi: A fudge-like candy made from thickened milk flavored with coconut, almond, or pistachio and served in small squares.

Candies like these are distributed on Eids and family occasions like birthdays. It is also a tradition that when something good happens—passing an examination at school, for example, or becoming a parent for the first time—one passes out candy as an offering to friends and neighbors.

CHEWING PAN

Pan ("PAHN") is a mixture of tobacco paste, various mixed spices, betel nut, and coconut attractively laid out on a green leaf that has been spread with a lime paste. All the ingredients are commonly found in Pakistan, except for the betel leaves, which still have to be imported from Bangladesh and Sri Lanka, despite increasing success in growing the plant in Sindh.

Pan is not available in restaurants as it does not function as a main dish or as an accompaniment. It is sold in shops that sell basic food items and soft drinks, in which a special counter facing the pavement is given over to the preparation of pan. More commonly, it is prepared and sold from a mobile street stand. People will often buy the pan to chew after a meal because it is said to aid the digestive process. The people who sell it are known as *pan wallahs*.

Pan wallahs have to work hard to make a living out of selling an inexpensive snack; a 16-hour day is not uncommon. The typical pan wallah squats on a small platform surrounded by colorful bottles containing the various ingredients. Special mixtures using less common ingredients are available from some pan wallahs, and for these more exotic pans a higher price is charged. While each vendor has his own style and recipes, the basic process is the same. He begins by taking in the palm of his hand one of his precut leaves and spreads a white lime paste on it. The various ingredients are added, and the final spread is then topped with a liquid syrup. The adept pan wallah then swiftly folds it into a compact little package. The customer places the little bundle in one side of the mouth and chews it slowly, allowing the various juices and flavors to work on the taste buds.

The presence of tobacco makes pan addictive, and it has become a daily habit for some people. The unmistakable marks of the habitual pan chewer are pale, yellowish-brown lips and teeth with a reddish-black lining. The coloring is unavoidable for anyone who regularly chews the preparation.

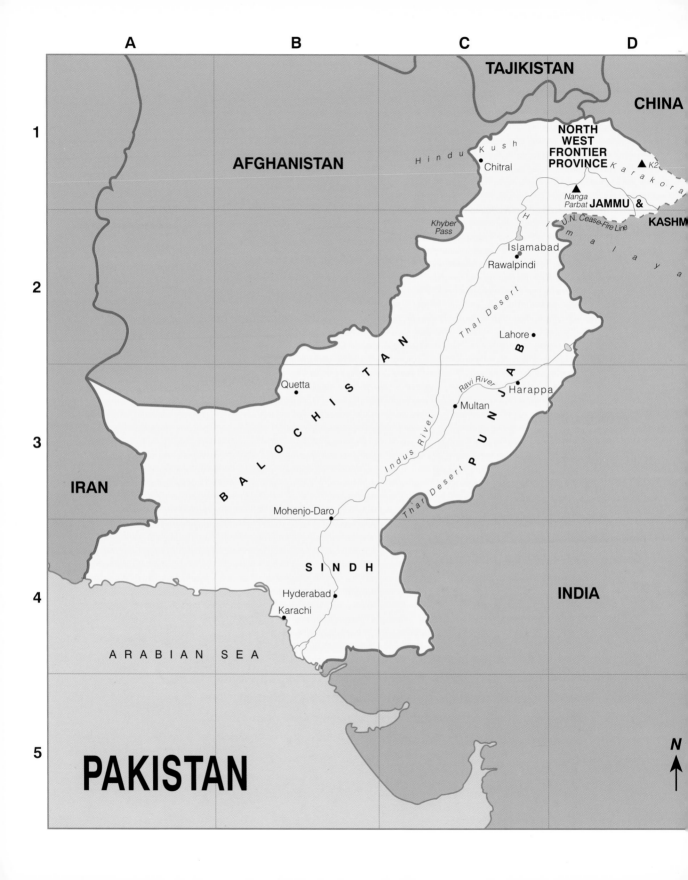

Balochistan   B3

Chitral   C1

Harappa   C3
Himalayas   D2
Hindu Kush   C1
Hyderabad   B4

Indus River   C3
Islamabad   C2

Jammu and Kashmir
   D1,D2

K2   D1
Karachi   B4
Karakorams   D1
Khyber Pass   C2

Lahore   C2

Mohenjo-Daro   B3
Multan   C3

Nanga Parbat   D1
North West Frontier
   Province   D1

Punjab   C3

Quetta   B3

Ravi River   C3
Rawalpindi   C2

Sindh   B4

Thal Desert   C2
Thar Desert   C3

U.N. Cease-Fire Line   D2

—— *International Boundary*

 Mountain

 Capital

 City

 River

Lake

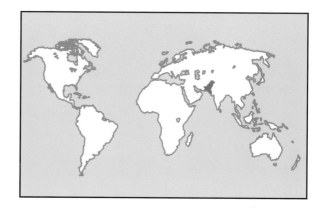

QUICK NOTES

OFFICIAL NAME
Islamic Republic of Pakistan

NATIONAL LANGUAGE
Urdu

STATE RELIGION
Islam

LAND AREA
307,374 square miles

MAIN GEOGRAPHIC FEATURES
Indus Plain and delta, Himalayas, Karakorams, Hindu Kush

HIGHEST POINT
Mt. K2 (28,251 feet)

MAJOR RIVER
Indus River (1,700 miles)

PROVINCES
Punjab, Sindh, Balochistan, North West Frontier Province, Jammu and Kashmir (disputed)

POPULATION
120 million

CAPITAL
Islamabad

CURRENCY
Pakistani Rupee ($1 = 26 Rs)

CHIEF PRODUCE
Wheat, sugarcane, millet, fruits

MAJOR POLITICAL LEADERS
Muhammad Ali Jinnah—Spearheaded the Partition on August 14, 1947. First leader of Pakistan.

Zulfikar Ali Bhutto—When elected prime minister in 1973, he reformed the educational and health systems. Deposed in 1977 and executed in 1979.

General Mohammad Zia ul-Haq—Declared martial law in 1977. Promised elections but was still in power when he died in 1988.

Benazir Bhutto—Daughter of Zulfikar Ali Bhutto, she was elected prime minister in 1988, the first woman leader of a modern Islamic state. She was ousted on charges of corruption in 1990, and has been a popular opposition leader since.

Nawaz Sharif—Elected prime minister in 1990 during elections widely believed to have been rigged. Deposed in April 1993 and reinstated a month later.

GLOSSARY

Ashura	("AH-shoo-rah") The 10th day of the first month of the Moslem calendar. On this day, Moslems commemorate the death of Hussein, Mohammad's grandson.
Azan	("a-ZAHN") The Moslem call to prayer, which is an announcement of the first Pillar of Faith.
burquah	("berh-KWAH") The robe and veil worn by traditional Moslem women that completely covers the body.
doab	("DOH-hb") The fertile area between the streams of the Indus in the south.
dupatta	("du-PEHT-tah") Long, narrow scarf worn with a *shalwar kamiz*.
garam masala	("geh-REHM meh-SAH-lah") Combination of roasted spices used as a basic ingredient in curries.
Haj	("HAHJ") Pilgrimage to Mecca, the spiritual center of Islam; a requirement for every Moslem and one of the five Pillars of Faith.
imam	Attendant of a mosque and prayer leader.
karez	("KAH-rez") Irrigation system in Balochistan where water is channeled. into underground tunnels and then drawn off into wells.
masjid	("MEHZ-jid") The Arabic and Urdu word for "mosque."
matchlocks	Gunlock that ignites the charge with a slow match.
melmastia	("mel-MAHS-tyah") The concept of hospitality to guests.
pan	("PAHN") Preparation of several ingredients, wrapped in a betel leaf, and chewed slowly.
Pukhtunwali	("PUHK-tuhn-wah-lee") The Pathan concept of honor by which they identify themselves.
purdah	("PERH-dah") The Pakistani custom, also found in other traditional Moslem communities, of keeping women in seclusion. Women in purdah wear the burquah in public.
Ramadan	("reh-meh-DAHN") The ninth month of the Moslem calendar, during which the faithful fast from sunrise to sunset.
urs	("OORS") Saints' death anniversary, when their communion with God is celebrated.

BIBLIOGRAPHY

Amin, Mohammad, Duncan Willetts and Graham Hancock. *Journey Through Pakistan*, Camerapix Publishers International, Nairobi, 1982.

Caldwell, John C. *Let's Visit Pakistan,* Burke Publishing Co., Bridgeport, Conn., 1985.

Cummings, P.D.: *Pakistan*, Wayland Publishing, Minneapolis, Minn., 1987.

Pakistan in Pictures, Lerner Publications, Minneapolis, Minn., 1989.

Weston, Mark. *The Land and People of Pakistan,* Harper Collins, Armonk, N.Y., 1992.

Yusufali, Jabeen. *Pakistan: An Islamic Treasure,* Dillon Press, Minneapolis, Minn., 1990.

INDEX

INDEX

INDEX

PICTURE CREDITS
APA: 4, 5, 6, 40, 41, 46, 67, 76, 77, 79, 110, 114, 120
Hulton-Deutsch: 24, 25
Hutchison Library: 7, 31, 39 (top), 47, 51, 64, 75, 90, 111
Richard I'Anson: 13, 72, 84, 86, 117, 118
Image Bank: 1, 8, 82, 85
Bjorn Klingwall: 17, 21, 52, 74, 78, 83, 103
Life File Photo Library: 3, 12, 16, 44, 49, 55, 58, 62, 63, 66, 81, 91, 97, 98, 123
Christine Osborne: 10, 11, 15, 19, 20, 22, 26, 30, 32, 33, 34, 35, 36, 37, 38, 39 (bottom), 42, 43, 50, 54, 56, 57, 59, 61, 65, 68, 69, 70, 71, 80, 87, 89, 92, 93, 96, 99, 102, 106, 108, 109, 112, 116, 119
Pakistan High Commission, Singapore: 23, 28, 29
Pakistan International Airlines: 53
Bernard Sonneville: 104, 107
Sunday Times, Singapore: 101